"Dr. Wahlberg has been an amazing help to me over the past four years that I have been going to him. I respect him for his honesty, understanding, and openness. I remember the first time I walked into his office, the first thing he did was show me a picture of his family, and name each person. I thought this was great because every other psychologist I have had would get very nervous, and change the subject if you would ask about their life outside their office. The way he handled that made me respect and trust him even more. I truly believe that I could not have gotten even 10% as far as I have without the help of Dr. Wahlberg."

~ Dan, 14 years old

"I've read dozens of books and tried countless techniques to manage my son's outbursts. Only after using Dr. Wahlberg's strategies have we seen results; our son is able to manage his emotions and control his behavior. Dr. Wahlberg understands how children with autism view the world and why they struggle with behavior and social interactions. His strategies get results because they are tailored to the unique needs of children on the spectrum. The behavior strategies outlined in this book have opened up a whole new world for our family. Daily meltdowns have been replaced with self-control and serenity. He has changed our lives!"

~ Carla Kemp, parent of a child on the spectrum

"In his book *Finding the Gray,* Dr. Wahlberg serves as an intermediary, explaining the meaningful differences between the clinical study of autism and the need for real-life results in the daily experiences of his patients. Parents and professionals alike will be able to harvest and apply useful information and strategies from the overwhelming amount of data that comprises current autism research. Resisting the temptation to view individuals with autism as just so many case studies, Dr. Wahlberg gets to the heart of the matter: those with autism are as deserving of human dignity and respect as anyone else. And they have the same right to find their path in an inhospitable world as the next person. *Finding the Gray* challenges the reader to make as much of an effort to understand how autism feels for those who have it as we ask those with autism to try to understand us. This is an important and very hopeful book."

~ Jennifer L. Bollero, Esq., attorney
and parent of a child on the spectrum

"Rarely does a book accomplish as much as *Finding the Gray.* In this excellent resource, Dr. Wahlberg has provided his readers a way to see the world through the eyes of Asperger's/autism spectrum disorder (ASD). He helps us understand the black and white world of persons with ASD and shows how their sensory awareness, perceptions, and particular logic direct their seemingly illogical actions. In a down-to-earth style, with many examples drawn from his years of experience with this disorder, Dr. Wahlberg offers both therapists and family members what they need to understand and respond to a person with ASD with less frustration and greater effectiveness. With hope and optimism, he teaches his readers to carry out practical management of social interactions and sensory challenges so that people with ASD can fulfill their potential to live happy, productive lives. It is a must-read for anyone who works or lives with a person on the spectrum."

     ~ Dr. Margaret Wehrenberg, author of the best-selling
     The 10 Best-Ever Anxiety Management Techniques and
     The 10 Best-Ever Depression Management Techniques

"Dr. Wahlberg has the unique ability to not only understand how the brain of an Asperger's child works, but he can explain it in clear, non-scientific terms that everyone can understand. Dr. Wahlberg relates to children who have Asperger's better than any professional we've ever worked with. His innate understanding comes across in this book; he writes in the same light, chatty style he uses one-on-one in his sessions with our son."

     ~Michael Simon, parent of a child on the spectrum

"As a parent of a child with Asperger's, I found Dr. Wahlberg's book to be a useful tool in figuring out how to better understand and guide my child. The examples were real life examples, ones I could relate to easily. The advice was straightforward and down to earth. A very practical approach to living with a child with Asperger's, the book has helped me understand Asperger's better and therefore be a better parent to my son."

     ~ Garey Schmidt, parent of a child on the spectrum

"Dr. Wahlberg has worked with our 14-year-old son who has Asperger's, and has been an extremely effective psychologist. His comfortable, easy, positive attitude and style quickly results in children and parents liking and respecting him, feeling liked and respected by him, and being willing to work with him. In our experience, Dr. Wahlberg very quickly recognizes, understands, and defines what is going on with children on the autism spectrum, and he provides children and parents with tools that result in steady improvement in the children's abilities to successfully interact with others and deal with their other challenges. For our son, Dr. Wahlberg's approach and techniques have dramatically improved our son's ability, desire, and self-confidence to interact with others and, in so many additional ways, to succeed as he is now doing in life."

~ Nancy Sohn, parent of a child on the spectrum

"Dr. Wahlberg has been invaluable in the success of my son's treatment for Asperger's (autism). My son had major anxiety and school issues. We began to see Dr. Wahlberg and he put together a plan that allowed my son to learn how to manage his anxiety and be a part of the school community. Without Dr. Wahlberg's vast knowledge of autism-related disorders, my son would not have achieved the success that he has. Thank you, Dr. Wahlberg!"

~ Mary Kay Betz, Marketing & Research Director
Unlocking Autism, Midwest Regional Representative
www.unlockingautism.org

Finding the Gray

Understanding and Thriving in the Black and White World of Autism and Asperger's

Timothy J. Wahlberg

Published by Wahlberg & Associates
Geneva, Illinois
www.findingthegray.com

Finding the Gray
Understanding and Thriving in the Black and White World of Autism and Asperger's

Copyright © 2010
by Timothy J. Wahlberg, Ph.D.

ISBN 13: 978-0-615-35704-1
ISBN 10: 0-615-35704-0
LCCN: 2010911446

Cover and Diagram Illustrations by Elissabeth Fehlman
Edited by Deborah McKew
Design and Layout by John Grossman, Back Channel Press

Published by Wahlberg & Associates
Geneva, Illinois
Printed in the United States of America

Publisher's Cataloging-in-Publication data

Wahlberg, Timothy J.

    Finding the gray : understanding and thriving in the black and white world of autism and Asperger's / Timothy J. Wahlberg.

    p. cm.

    ISBN 978-0-615-35704-1

    1. Autistic children --Care. 2. Parents of autistic children. 3. Autistic Disorder. 4. Autism. 5. Autistic Disorder --rehabilitation. 6. Autism in children. 7. Asperger's syndrome. 8. Asperger Syndrome. I. Title.

RC553.A88 .W34 2010
616.85/8832—22   2010911446

DEDICATION

This book is dedicated to my three beautiful daughters:
Elli, Gia, and Cece.

Putting this book together was an amazing experience. I feel very fortunate to do what I do every day. I would like to thank all of the families with whom I have been privileged to work over the years; they have helped me create a certain level of understanding for those on the spectrum.

CONTENTS

PREFACE

Stevie was 2½ years old. His mother told me not to interact with him, just to sit on the other side of the room so he could get used to me being there. I had done a lot of volunteer work with kids (things like the Big Brother/Big Sister Program, coaching, etc.), so I had experience with children, but not with autism. I sat there and watched. It was as if I were invisible! There was no interaction and no acknowledgement whatsoever from Stevie. That was 1995. I was a graduate student, and I had never even heard the term autism before.

In my very first graduate class, I was given a flier advertising a job for someone to work as an in-home therapist with Stevie. A young and willing student, I was excited to work in my field of study and I jumped on the chance to go for the interview. After that first meeting, I was hired by Stevie's family and trained in applied behavior analysis (ABA).

Nothing could have prepared me for the first day we implemented ABA with Stevie; I had never heard such a scream before. My immediate thought was, "I cannot do this!" But within five minutes, he was responding to my commands, although minimally, and while he was still screaming. Eventually, he responded so well to treatment that he had a successful run in public school and is now gearing up to start college. I ended up working with Stevie for two years as an in-home therapist, and that changed the course of my career and my life forever.

I learned so much while working with him that I ultimately began working for other families with children on the autism spectrum and I started seeing clients in the Community Clinic at Saint Xavier University in Chicago. After my experience with Stevie, I was so intrigued to learn more about autism that I could not stop thinking about it, reading about it, and studying it; it became my passion and I have not stopped studying it ever since.

One day, my graduate school advisor, Dr. Rotatori, asked me what I thought was going on inside Stevie's head. "What is he thinking?" he asked me. I thought to myself, "I do not know, but I want to try and figure this out." That was the beginning of 15 years of work with autism that has brought me to the point of writing this book. I have spent my professional life devoted to studying autism, Asperger's disorder and autism spectrum disorder (ASD).

I do not have a child on the autism spectrum; I did not have any children when I began this journey. Today, I have three beautiful daughters, Elli (11), Gia (10) and Cece (8), whom I adore, and who also give me a baseline to understand how children on the autistic spectrum are different. I have treated hundreds of children on the spectrum, and I see approximately 50 to 60 each week in my office. I feel very fortunate to do what I do. My job is never boring and is filled with challenges. In the past two years, I have founded the Prairie Clinic, in Geneva, Illinois, where we specialize in treating children on the spectrum and the families of the children on the spectrum.

A clinical psychologist and a school psychologist, I speak both regionally and nationally, educating parents on autism and Asperger's Disorder. I have given hundreds of presentations on autism, and written and published academic articles and books on autism, but I have never written anything specifically for the parents and educators who work with these unique individuals. This book is intended for all of you parents who have children on the spectrum, and also for teachers, professionals, and caregivers who work with children on the spectrum, but who do not know where, or how, to start to help them.

When families first receive a diagnosis of autism it can be devastating. I have given the diagnosis for more than a decade and have worked with hundreds of parents who were referred to me because they had just received the painful and frightening diagnosis of autism. I have experienced their suffering and desperation first hand as they become aware of the possible implications. Often, all they are told is, "Your child is on the autism spectrum…good luck," and they are sent on their way without further help. Many are left to ask the question, "Well, now what?" This book is the now what—a guide map to begin the process of understanding and adapting to this new reality.

When parents google autism and get 30 million hits, they come to my office and ask, "What do I read? Where do I start?" Start here, with this book, to begin to step inside the world of autism, to begin to understand the unique perspective on the world these people have, and to begin to understand their unique way of processing the world. Diagnosis, although painful, opens the doors to better understanding and new treatment possibilities. There is a lot of hope.

Years of research and clinical observation have led me to develop a theory of what autism is and how people who are on the autistic spectrum see the world. However, the purpose of this book is not to focus on the research; the purpose is to help readers—parents, educators, therapists—identify and respond positively to people on the spectrum.

This book provides both a starting place to increase your understanding of autism and a resource for realistic ideas on how to teach children who are on the spectrum to be more functional and more successful. Many parents have gone around in circles, working diligently with doctors and therapists, achieving seemingly little gain because the autism was missed. Being aware and understanding autism changes that. Hopefully, this book will provide that moment of, "Aha! I get it now…their world is starting to make sense."

In order to respond in a positive way, it is important to know how individuals on the spectrum think and process the world around them. You will come to see that the way they see things is not wrong; it's just different. When you understand that difference, and how it impacts the child, you can begin to understand his experience and his world. Once you can enter into that world, change begins to take place and your child will become more functional and better able to manage the world around him. As you grow in your understanding, you will learn that your child on the spectrum has a personality first and autism second. Children with autism are people just like us, facing problems just like we do.

Children on the spectrum have, first and foremost, a social disability. This book presents a clear picture of the why behind this, along with techniques to teach them to overcome this challenge and ultimately persevere in a very social society and social world. My objective is that this book will help you to see that picture fully, gain a solid understanding of autism, and, ultimately, experience more success in shaping your child into a happy and functional adult. Happy and functional. That is my goal for these exceptional people.

For the most part, these are very smart individuals. Teaching them how their brains work and how to be functional in the very flexible, dynamic world in which they live is pivotal to their ability to be successful. I accomplish this by focusing on their relative strengths and using those strengths to supplement areas in which they struggle. Their world is not easy; they are forced to deal with significant challenges every day. They need to learn how to master those obstacles in order to prosper in the world. If we can teach them how to be more social, how to overcome their tendency to think in black and white extremes, and how to live life in the middle ground, they can achieve as much as anyone without autism.

There are many stories in this book that are based on composites of the children and families that I have worked with over the years. Most of them describe higher functioning individuals on the spectrum, although I feel this book and its content applies to all individuals on the spectrum, including those more severely impacted by autism spectrum disorder. My intent was to capture an accurate characterization of an individual on the spectrum that could be applied to someone of any age. I have attempted to describe the guiding concepts that 15 years of providing therapy have proven to be useful in understanding someone on the spectrum. As a result, I have needed to revisit certain topics in order to describe them from different perspectives and as they relate to different exceptionalities.

There is incredible hope for these individuals who are so talented, bright, and autistic. Working with them is extremely gratifying. Seeing therapeutic change, watching individuals and families learn to persevere and to take the gifts these children possess and use them to their children's advantage, and improving their ability to function in our social world, is very rewarding.

Those who succeed in life do "find the gray" area when they learn to compromise and be flexible. They then can go out into the world functionally embracing all of life—including the middle ground between the extremes. As a result of that increasing functionality, they can play the game of life and win!

CHAPTER 1

THE WORLD OF AUTISM: LIFE TIMES 10

I have spoken to thousands of incredibly loving, committed parents since I started working with individuals on the spectrum. I hear their pain, frustration, and aggravation.

*I*ndividuals with autism spectrum disorder (ASD) represent a very perplexing and fascinating phenomenon. They exhibit exceptional proficiency in a number of areas, especially those that are more linear and data driven in nature, such as remembering detailed factual information, memorizing lists, and using computers. They also struggle in a number of areas, especially from a social standpoint. In particular, they have difficulty with communication, especially social/emotional communication, and they can be obsessed with rituals or objects. They can hyperfocus on a certain topic and can get stuck on routines. Most importantly, they have difficulty interacting and functioning socially.

DEFINITION OF THE AUTISTIC SPECTRUM

The term *autistic spectrum* is an umbrella term that indicates the presence of specific diagnostic criteria. Although there are three specific diagnostic categories under the spectrum umbrella—autism, Asperger's disorder, and PDD/NOS (which stands for pervasive development disorders–not otherwise specified)—anyone who meets the basic criteria is said to be *on the spectrum,* or to have ASD.

The autism spectrum includes individuals who are *high functioning* (in which the disorder is almost undetectable) to those who are very *low functioning* (they are unable to carry out some, or most, of life's basic skills and, as a result, may need constant supervision). While the general theory and principals in this book apply regardless of where someone falls on the spectrum, this book is primarily geared toward treatment of higher functioning children.

Autism, as a category, is the most pervasive diagnostic category on the spectrum. That is to say, children with this diagnosis are the most significantly impacted in their abilities to function in daily life. These kids might not speak, might have extreme sensory issues, and might also have significant social impairment. Higher functioning autism is not a diagnostic category, but implies that the child's cognitive (intellectual, innate ability) functioning is in the average range or higher. Moving up the spectrum toward increasing functionality, a child who does not meet the criteria for autism would be diagnosed as having Asperger's disorder.

The difference diagnostically between autism and Asperger's disorder lies within the child's language development. Unlike individuals with autism, children with Asperger's disorder develop language within the developmentally appropriate age range. PDD-NOS is the diagnosis that is given to children who do not strictly meet the criteria for autism or Asperger's disorder, but who are considered to be in the PDD (pervasive developmental disorders) diagnostic category.

Intelligence can vary significantly in individuals on the spectrum, so IQ is not an effective diagnostic criterion. I have treated kids with IQs that range from the 70s to well over 130 or more. Some research indicates that 60–70% of those diagnosed with autism have cognitive impairment, i.e., an IQ below 75. However, I do not believe these statistics for a number of reasons.

First, individuals with autism process the world differently than *neuro-typical* individuals (those considered to have normal brain functioning—see Chapter 4, How Autism Develops), and therefore do not perform as well on tests standardized for neuro-typical individuals. Second, the contexts in which such evaluations are given do not bode well for individuals on the spectrum. During the intellectual assessment process, examinees are required to take a test that is presented using verbal directions, given by a person with whom they are not familiar, and held in an unfamiliar environment. In addition, most individuals on the autism spectrum learn better visually than they do verbally. These are all factors that could impact test performance and resulting scores.

Finally, individuals on the autistic spectrum are motivated primarily by extrinsic factors rather than intrinsic factors. Intrinsic motivation is social, extrinsic motivation is not. Therefore, it is unlikely that a child on the spectrum would want to do well during the examination in order to please the examiner. All of these factors stack the deck against the child on the autistic spectrum from testing well, so some caution should be exercised in using traditional IQ scores for evaluation. Many individuals on the spectrum are extremely gifted in areas that do not reveal themselves on a standardized IQ test.

One thing is generally accepted among professionals treating individuals on the spectrum—every person embodies a unique combination of strengths and challenges. While there are commonalities, there is no one-size-fits-all description of someone on the spectrum.

AUTISM IS LIFE TIMES 10

Autism is not a mental illness and it is not a disease. As I have just mentioned above, the fact that a person has autism does not necessarily mean that that person has a low IQ. People with autism process the world differently. These individuals take in and process information on a neurological level differently than the majority of us. Their way is not wrong, it's just different, and that creates difficulty for them in a world geared toward the majority and therefore suited for people with normal neurological processing. Once you understand this aspect of autism, or Asperger's disorder, it is much easier to interact with these individuals, to speak with them, and to plan interventions to help them.

So what is different about children on the spectrum? I believe that children on the spectrum are just like you and me in many ways. They have the same feelings, the same emotions, the same desires, interests, and dreams. Like children who are neuro-typical, children with autism represent a broad range of personality types. The difference is that they have difficulty processing the sensory stimulation from their environment and that can affect the expression of their personalities.

Human beings absorb and process information from our environment through sensory perception. Our brains and bodies receive sensations through perceptive fields including: visual (sight), tactile (touch), auditory (hearing), olfactory (smell), taste buds (taste), gastrointestinal (food ingestion), the sensory motor system (movement of our limbs), vestibular (balance), proprioceptive (the body's awareness of where your limbs are in space); and kinesthetic (the sensation of movement of muscles, tendons, and joints). In addition, humans process information through another channel—social engagement—that involves a combination of other senses (there is much more on this in later chapters).

The way children with autism struggle to process sensory stimulation can manifest in varying degrees. Some children come into the world and find it over-stimulating; they can be extremely sensitive to sounds, light, and touch. They might experience sensory motor difficulties or gastrointestinal (stomach) sensitivities. They may experience challenges in any one of their sensory modalities. These sensitivities require energy to manage, and that energy demand reduces the amount of energy left to process interpersonal encounters and their social environment.

Imagine if there was too much stimulation in the room where you are right now. Imagine if it was too loud, or if the lights were too bright, or if the temperature was 85 degrees and you had on a wool sweater. Could you process what you are reading? Probably not. This is what is going on with kids on the spectrum, only their experience isn't just a little enhanced, it is 10 times what the rest of us experience. In many cases, autistic behavior (e.g., rocking, screaming, or zoning out) begins to manifest as a way to cope with this uncomfortable over-stimulation.

I use the phrase *times 10* to remind parents that kids on the spectrum face the same problems as everyone else, but their autism magnifies their issues by a factor of 10. Many people have sensory issues; kids with autism have them times 10. Many people struggle socially, but with autism, it is times 10. In spite of that fact, these kids have the ability to grow and learn and develop just like everyone else.

I have very high expectations for all the kids I treat. As soon as we meet a goal, I raise the bar again. But we have to be careful when it comes to some of our expectations of them socially. There are some things they just cannot and do not want to do in that area. Since they struggle with interacting and functioning socially, we have to be careful of what our expectations are when it comes to their level of social understanding.

PERSONALITIES FIRST, DIAGNOSIS SECOND

There are as many different personalities in the autistic community as there are among neuro-typical individuals. Kids on the spectrum can be introverted or extroverted; they can express all different types of personalities. A diagnosis of ASD does not define a child's personality, it just defines his processing method and his way of perceiving the world. These kids have personalities first and autism or Asperger's disorder second.

Every child is different—as the saying goes, "If you have met one person with Asperger's disorder, you have met one person with Asperger's disorder." No two children have the same issues or present their issues to the same degree. Each child is a unique mixture of challenges and gifts. That's part of what makes diagnosis and treatment challenging.

Individuals on the spectrum need to embrace the strengths that they have and use those strengths to help them learn to function in areas that are challenging to them. They need to acknowledge their autism and learn to manage it so that they can persevere and prosper in a social society.

HAPPY AND FUNCTIONAL

Individuals with ASD can and do live productive and satisfying lives. As parents, educators, and therapists, we have to be very careful of the lifestyles we impose, or want to impose, on these individuals. Their lives may not fit neatly into our preconceived notions of what their lifestyles should be, but that does not mean that these individuals cannot be successful. My goal for my clients is to help them become happy and functional. I do not make value judgments about what they do with their lives.

I want to make sure that they can go online and handle a transaction with the bank. I want to make sure that when their boss says, "Hey, can you stop doing what you're doing and come over here and help me?" they can do it. I want to make sure that they can shop at a grocery store, fill a prescription, call for a doctor's appointment, or fill their cars with gas if they drive. That's what I mean by functional.

THE INCREASE IN INCIDENCE

What has caused the increase in incidence of ASD over the past decade? In October of 2009, the Center for Disease Control published new statistics indicating that 1 in every 110 children is on the autism spectrum.

There are several factors that could potentially be contributing to the increase in both the incidence and the diagnosis of spectrum disorders. It is beyond the scope of this book to begin to disseminate the reasons for the increase in incidence, but I do believe that there are more children on the spectrum than there were 10 to 15 years ago.

Many studies indicate that autism may not only be on the rise, but it may be that Asperger's disorder and PDD–NOS kids who weren't previously recognized are now being identified. Better diagnosticians, using clearer criteria than ever before, may also be less hesitant to issue the diagnosis of autism spectrum disorder because the stigma is lessening every day as more is understood.

I believe that someone is either born with autistic processing or is not. There are many theories about why this happens. My purpose in this book, however, is not to debate why autism happens. My purpose is to provide more understanding of autism spectrum disorder, and, with that foundation, to also provide experience-based techniques that offer hope and support to anyone dealing with kids on the spectrum; the goal is for these kids to be happy and functional in a society not built for them.

PARENTING A CHILD ON THE SPECTRUM

Parenting a child on the spectrum is one of the toughest parenting jobs on the planet. Parents need to understand how and what their kids are thinking in order to be able to parent effectively. Traditional parenting techniques may not be effective, and might even be counter productive, skyrocketing the anxiety level of the child.

One parent said it this way:

> I would just force my son to go to school, because that is what good parents do. But by demanding he go without my understanding what he was experiencing, I was simply pushing him toward the very things that were causing his anxiety (which were the social challenges he was experiencing, as well as the stress of doing what he did not want to do, such as homework). Once I understood and could address his discomfort with school, I was able to get him to school without causing

him further distress. By the same token, I used to allow less structure around him because it seemingly made him so uncomfortable. Today, I know that this structure is what helps him make sense of what is going on around him. I used to push when I should have pulled, and pulled when I should have pushed. Understanding autism has helped me to be a much more effective parent to my son.

Parenting any child can be a full time job, but it is even harder to parent a child on the spectrum. Family dynamics have an influence on these kids. There are siblings and other demands on any parent's time. Many parents end up in survival mode, becoming tired and worn out from the constant demands on their time and energy and then taking action that feeds the autism, instead of taking action that promotes better mental and emotional health. One mother said to me, "If I did all I needed to do, I would never be able to make dinner." Parents need to realize that sometimes we cannot do it all; we can only do what we are capable of doing, and that's okay.

There is an upside to parents having other demands on their time and energy. The absence of constant attention might also serve to increase the ability of a child on the spectrum to handle more on her own. It is a difficult balance, but it is important that we do not overparent exceptional children. In order to be functional adults, they need to learn to do things on their own, and reaching our limits as parents may provide an opportunity for them to learn both problem solving and coping skills.

I have spoken to thousands of incredibly loving, committed parents since I started working with individuals on the spectrum. I hear their pain, frustration, and aggravation when working with their children. I also see their joy when they accomplish real growth. Parenting a child on the spectrum is a daunting and never-ending task. I get it, even though I have not lived it.

I live with a very traditional sense of parental authority in my household. At this point, my preteen daughters are motivated to please me; they also respect my authority. I know that at some point during adolescence it will be natural for them to challenge that authority as they begin to develop their independence. It is a much different twist with someone who is on the spectrum who may not always understand the authority relationship that a child has with his parents when he lives at home. Kids on the spectrum do not understand why they have to do things at home that they do not want to do; they may not always be motivated to please their parents.

HOW HARD SHOULD YOU PUSH A CHILD ON THE SPECTRUM?

When we ask younger children on the spectrum to behave in a particular way (e.g., sit quietly, be polite, stop fidgeting, pay attention), their reactions can be very painful to watch: crying, screaming, and squirming. So, how much stress are we going to force on a child when we see that this is very difficult for them? The challenge is that all of these kids are seeing and processing things differently, and every parent or educator has a different tolerance level for enduring this behavior; the line of how much stress is too much is very fluid depending upon the situation.

Therapeutic intervention requires some pushing to create change. Inevitably, the child is going to respond by being upset when she doesn't get to do what she wants to do. All kids can experience these issues, but for children on the spectrum, who are more challenged by difficult situations due to their issues in processing the environment, it is even tougher for them to navigate (times 10). As a result, they can get into problematic situations more quickly than children not on the spectrum. When you engage in treatment, you take a theoretical and moral leap, believing that you know what's best for the child in the long run—this is what drives interventions.

Working with children on the spectrum is a balancing act. Trying to make a child do something he doesn't want to do when he's totally confused and totally overloaded is fruitless. I try to teach give and take. If I can motivate a child to engage in the activity he doesn't want to do, then I'll allow him an opportunity to do what he does want to do. Over time, we can reduce some of that abrasive reaction to an event or activity. I really don't try to cause the kids a lot of pain or discomfort, but I also have to teach them that sometimes we all have to do things that we do not want to do.

Often, the parents need to grasp that concept as well. Many parents need to learn to set and enforce boundaries so that their children on the spectrum will learn to do things that they may not want to do (see Chapter 14, Creating Effective Strategies/Interventions). In the larger world, this is an important life skill that allows us to be functional.

CHAPTER 2

THE CONTROL THEORY

The control theory explains how autism develops, as well as provides an explanation as to the reasons behind autistic behavior.

*I*n a neuro-typical individual, multiple sensory systems all work together to absorb, process, organize, and integrate information in order for the person to function. In individuals on the autistic spectrum, any of these systems can be affected to varying degrees. Those with higher functioning autism may only experience a moderate level of difficulty in one or two of these sensory systems; those with lower functioning autism may be more severely affected in most or all of these systems.

What is very promising within the field of neurology is that we no longer have a Darwinian concept of neurological development. Neurons were once thought to die off if they were not activated early on in life, but we are starting to believe that this is not the case. We can stimulate neurons to fire, and thus stimulate interconnectivity. We have also discovered that other parts of the brain can and will take over various functions for damaged parts of the brain.

THEORIES OF AUTISM

There are several recognized theories that attempt to shed some light on areas of deficit for those on the autistic spectrum. Three of the most popular and well researched are described below:

1. Theory of Mind—Theory of mind is the ability one has to attribute mental states, e.g., beliefs or attitudes, to oneself and to others and to understand that others have beliefs and attitudes that are different from one's own. Research suggests that children at about age 4 or 5 begin to develop a sense that they think differently from others. The theory of mind approach proposes that individuals with ASD do not understand that other people have differing perspectives compared to their own. Theory of mind also supposes that an individual with ASD has trouble accepting that other people's thoughts differ from his own or even that people can think and feel differently about various situations.

2. Central Coherence Theory—At about the same time children typically begin to develop theory of mind, they are also developing the ability to integrate pieces of information into a coherent whole, known as central coherence. The central coherence theory postulates that the ability to be flexible and incorporate unpredictability is compromised in an individual with ASD. Thus, a person with autism tends to focus on too much detail and overlooks the whole concept, often missing context. This is the proverbial can't-see-the-forest-for-the-trees perspective.

3. Executive Functioning Deficits Theory—Executive functioning is the ability to make decisions. The human brain takes about 25 years to fully develop this ability. The executive functioning deficits theory postulates that individuals with autism have difficulty learning from past experiences (a function of the frontal lobe). This impedes their ability to make decisions and form patterns of behavior based on incorporating any new information. As a result, they are inflexible, black and white thinkers.

THE CONTROL THEORY OF AUTISM

Based on my extensive research and observations over years of clinical experience, I have developed a different theory, *the control theory*, which I believe is a more accurate and complete explanation of autism.[1]

The control theory explains how autism develops, as well as provides an explanation as to the reasons behind autistic behavior. The theory of mind, central coherence, and executive functioning deficits theories cannot address the issues of younger children because they would not yet have developed those behavioral, emotional, and cognitive (thinking) skills that are considered by these theories to be weak, even if they are not on the spectrum. Although these theories accurately describe some areas of deficit for those on the spectrum, they do not offer an explanation as to why these issues develop in those on the spectrum. Therefore, there is a big gap when using those theories to explain the autism of younger children.

While other theories present the disorder as a *breakdown* of an underlying neural mechanism, the control theory of autism explains the disorder as the *developmental emergence* of a functionally distinct neuro-behavioral architecture. In other words, the brain of a child with autism develops differently, not wrong necessarily, from what is considered neuro-typical, or normal, development. People with autism are hardwired differently; they process the world differently and they function differently.

Normal neuro-behavioral architectures (or brain hardwiring and development) grow in a manner geared toward incorporating more and more complex forms of unpredictability, while autistic architectures develop toward reducing the very unpredictability that the typical architecture is attempting to incorporate. The control theory explains the development of this autistic architecture at a neurological level and

---

1   Wahlberg, Tim (2001). Autistic Spectrum Disorders: Educational and Clinical Interventions. In Anthony F. Rotatori, (Ed.), Advances in Special Education (Chapter 1). New York: JAI Elsevier Science.

ties this development to the behavioral manifestations, characteristics, and cognitive difficulties resulting from the irregular neurological development. (See Chapter 4 for more information on neuro-typical development.)

The Control Theory

The control theory of autism states that individuals are born having difficulty processing incoming sensory stimulus as a whole and therefore develop autism as a neurological and behavioral response designed to control/manage the incoming stimulus to either: 1) make sense of information from the environment; or 2) simply make it tolerable.

By necessity, as a child grows, brain development continues in response to environmental stimulation. Due to the fundamental neurological processing difference in the autistic brain, which impedes interconnectivity, (i.e., the neurons communicating—see Chapter 4, How Autism Develops), the individual's perception and interpretation of the environmental stimulus is limited or forced into very black and white, or concrete, terms.

This style of information processing becomes a pattern that is designed to limit, simplify, manage, and control the incoming information. The inability of the brain to automatize to the stimulation, that is, to process information without conscious effort, taxes the brain's resources. The overload caused by this shortage of resources inhibits the development of higher functioning processes (especially social), and gives rise to autistic behavior as a means to respond to or compensate for this inhibited development, ultimately resulting in a social disability called autism.

If the sensory environment is either overbearing or too complicated to understand, and the brain takes a turn from perceiving to tuning out, then the amount of communication between neurons is limited because of the difficulty involved in perception, in and of itself. In other words, the brain begins to limit the amount of sensory information allowed in, which further compromises the development of neurological interconnectivity. As a result, the neurological branching out of neurons to speak with one another becomes truncated, which leads to lack of flexibility. Thus, where interconnectivity grows automatically in those individuals without ASD, it is developing in the opposite direction in those with ASD (this will make more conceptual sense in the section on how individuals with ASD think and process information which is explained in Chapter 6, Spectrum Development).

The degree to which an individual experiences overstimulation may have a direct impact on the degree to which that individual develops ASD. This can be a very complex issue because the human body receives input from multiple senses at once; there could be sensitivity to one source or all of this input. In addition, the tolerance level for sensory input varies from one individual to another.

Based on the control theory of autism, it would make sense that individuals with autism would suffer in any, if not all, of the areas suggested by the other theories. If an individual is having trouble processing sensory information such as touch, light, sound, taste, and smell, and as a result, he is neurologically (in brain function, not in conscious awareness) forced to develop strategies to deal with this processing problem, it would follow that areas that involve a higher level of conceptualization would be compromised, as suggested by all three theories.

For instance, since individuals with autism are not processing social interactions at a young age in the same fashion as individuals without autism, the automatic process of social comparison does not occur in the same fashion as it does with those who do not have ASD. If this system is not functioning, it would make conceptual sense that the individual's ability to develop an intact theory of mind (the ability to see that there are other points of view) would be compromised, therefore causing trouble accepting the thoughts and ideas of other people when those thoughts and ideas differ from his own, as the theory of mind approach suggests.

It would also make conceptual sense that if one's ability to be flexible and incorporate unpredictability was not developed as the control theory suggests, it would be hard for one to collect a number of facts or bits of information and piece them together into the collective whole (i.e., weak central coherence, or inability to comprehend the big picture). I remember explaining this idea to a young man with higher functioning autism. I told him that sometimes it is difficult for an individual with autism to see the forest within the trees. I went on to explain that individuals with autism will not only suffer in this way, but they may see the leaves on the trees within the forest rather than the whole forest or the trees. This young man understood exactly what I was saying; he felt that, based on his perception of the world, he would see a caterpillar on the leaf on the tree and miss the forest!

The executive functioning deficits theory postulates that individuals with autism have difficulty learning from past experiences, which impedes their ability to make future decisions and develop patterns of behavior based on new information. One of the ways we become better at tasks is not only to practice them, but to learn from them. If an individual is inflexible and unable to learn from past experiences, then it would indicate that she is a very concrete, black and white thinker. This would fit with the control theory's postulation that black and white thinking is a result of sensory overload or sensory processing difficulties.

Unlike all of the other theories, the control theory explains the cause for autistic behavior with its supposition that the development of autistic neurology (and the resulting behavior associated with autism) is caused by the individual's need to control the stimuli being received from the environment around him. This theory also encompasses the main concepts of all the other theories, which are limited to describing the aftereffects of autism and do not address the underlying cause for its development. After working with kids with autism for more than 15 years, I find that the control theory is the theory that best explains the multitude of behaviors presented in autism, the characteristic manifestations of autism, and the reason behind them.

CHAPTER 3

WHAT DIFFERENCE CAN A DIAGNOSIS MAKE?

I have seen many, many kids misdiagnosed, or diagnosed with another disorder that does not effectively encompass all the issues that a diagnosis of spectrum disorder would include.

Having the proper diagnosis can make the difference between getting results and not getting results in therapy. If you suspect that your child has issues that are not being addressed through her current therapy, seek a diagnosis from a professional who is trained in working with children on the spectrum and therefore will know what to look for. This professional may have a very different interpretation of the child's behaviors and the issues he faces. I have seen many, many kids misdiagnosed, or diagnosed with another disorder that does not effectively encompass all the issues that a diagnosis of spectrum disorder would include. Autism spectrum disorders are relatively new diagnoses, but these diagnoses are becoming more common as more is understood about autism.

One young man I treat was put through a full two-day battery of tests at one of the most well known institutions in the Midwest; he was ultimately given the diagnosis "quirky." The professionals there found him engaging and funny in a one-to-one interaction; he was able to look them in the eye and carry on a conversation with the adult staff. Yet, he was suspended from school five times last year for incidences related to peer interactions that went wrong. He has a social disability.

Since he has been treated at the Prairie Clinic, he has been rediagnosed. Having worked with this young man and his family in private therapy for more than two years, I know for certain that he has Asperger's disorder. Treating him for ASD has proved very successful in helping him to learn skills necessary to navigate junior high school.

Today, even though most people who don't understand ASD would still find him quirky, his anxiety level has been dramatically reduced because he was properly diagnosed and treated; his family reports significant social strides, with steady improvements. His grades, which continue to climb, are beginning to reflect his true intellectual ability. No longer trapped in his own world by his inability to understand and function in the social world, he has begun to operate effectively, and, therefore, prosper in the real world. He has learned to play the game of life on life's terms.

It's an unfortunate fact, but far too common an experience, that even one of the best neurological centers in the country would see his behavior as simply quirky, bypassing the diagnosis that ultimately helped him to find the type of therapy he needs to treat his disability.

An in-depth discussion of possible misdiagnoses is important, but that is a sidebar from the main purpose of this book. I have presented much more information on the diagnostic process in Appendix A, including a listing of common misdiagnoses. If you are still in the diagnostic process, or if the treatment you are pursuing based on the current diagnoses is not producing results, please take the time to refer to that section.

CHAPTER 4

HOW AUTISM DEVELOPS

Neurological interconnectivity impacts flexibility, executive functioning, and processing of everything except the most finite, black and white data. The lack of interconnectivity is what causes the thinking of someone on the spectrum to seem rigid and compartmentalized.

What happens during "normal" child development? What happens differently to children on the spectrum? Normal is a touchy word today. No one is sure what constitutes normal development, but for the purpose of this book, let's call any child who is not on the autistic spectrum, one who is neuro-typical, normal. To make sense of the difficulties a child with ASD experiences, it's important to first have an understanding of neurological, biological, and physiological development—human hardwiring.

HUMAN HARDWIRING

Newborn babies are bombarded with sensory stimulation via all their senses from the moment they are born. When they leave the womb, a place that accommodates every sensory need perfectly, they are exposed to all sorts of higher level sensory stimuli. They have developed these senses in the womb, but when they are born, they are tasting, touching, and smelling the world. They are flooded with visual, gastrointestinal, vestibular, sensory motor, and proprioceptive stimuli, among others. Immediately, a newborn infant begins to experience, regulate, and process this incoming sensory information in order to make sense of her surrounding environment. No one has to teach us to process and make sense of our environment; we just do it because that is how our brains are built. That is the nature of human hardwiring.

DIFFERENTIATION

At birth, our brain contains billions of *neurons*, tiny nerve cells that process stimuli. When we are born, we learn and adapt to our surroundings; the neurons differentiate, which means that they become efficient at receiving and interpreting certain types of data. A neuron differentiated to take in and process language, for example, will not suddenly begin to process incoming olfactory stimuli. A neuron only fires (becomes active) when it receives the specific stimulus that it was differentiated to process. During the early stages of neurological development and differentiation, the autistic brain and the brain of a neuro-typical child begin to develop differently.

The brain of a child who is not on the spectrum is continually absorbing and organizing as much sensory information as possible. This is an automatic process; it is what the human brain is naturally hardwired to do. This process becomes cyclical and cumulative. The child craves new input which, in turn, differentiates neurons to be receptive to information and creates a pattern of growth and development that leads exponentially to an ever-increasing capacity for information. As the brain's capacity to manage information grows, the amount of information that the brain can process increases. The more information the brain can process and integrate, the easier it will be for the individual to adapt to a constantly changing sensory environment. The brain of a neuro-typical child thus becomes an information-processing machine, building its capability by experience, ultimately making it possible for the child to develop a healthy, flexible capacity for dealing with the world.

The process of differentiation is different for the child on the spectrum who, from the moment of birth, may experience varying degrees of difficulty managing sensory input and processing the environment. Instead of absorbing and processing the sensory stimulation, the neurons in the brain of someone on the spectrum can actually develop to block out the stimulation that is causing discomfort or even pain.

These neurons, now differentiated to block the uncomfortable stimuli, serve to limit the development of the brain because they are not receptive to new information. This process creates a cycle designed for self-preservation—the neurons systematically block out new information, reducing incoming stimuli and thus limiting development.

This need to control or manage sensory stimulation from the environment compounds upon itself to create an ever-decreasing desire for new input and stimulation, which ultimately has an impact on the behavior of the child and gives rise to some of the most common autistic behaviors. As a result, children on the spectrum will try to control the amount or the type of input in their environment to create consistency, which is calming to them. For example, they may spin the wheel of a toy car, watch the same video over and over, look repeatedly at the same book, or compulsively line up objects. This behavior is called *stimming* (derived from the word stimulus), which refers to any repeated behavior that calms the child.

In therapy, we are constantly working to keep the mind of a child with autism in an expanding growth mode, rather than allowing him to rigidly block out or shut down stimulus. By forcing the child, through exposure and repetition, to process unwanted stimuli, we are helping him strengthen the neural pathways. As the neural pathways strengthen, the child becomes more flexible and able to deal with inconsistencies in the environment.

I have been asked if a child on the spectrum can get worse. My answer is that the autism doesn't get worse, but that some of an individual's behavior can become more inflexible, which may make him appear as if he is getting worse. This is at least partially related to the child's neurology. Regressive behavior can manifest itself in an individual on the spectrum for a variety of reasons, for example, sensory overload or a change in his environment.

INTERCONNECTIVITY IN THE BRAIN

Billions of neurons, or nerve cells, move information to other neurons throughout the various parts of the brain. These are many more than we actually use in our lifetime. Even before a child is born, all the nerve cells he will ever possess have been formed. These nerve cells are like a mass of unconnected electrical wires. As the child grows and develops, his brain will constantly strive to connect the wires.

When we learn something new—how to ride a bike, tie our shoes, or speak a language—the brain differentiates neurons to create the impulses that cause the muscle movements that result in the body making the physical motions we know as "riding a bike," for example. Thus the brain forms an interconnected pathway for every task we learn.

As we practice riding the bike, the pathway becomes stronger and the messages move faster, resulting in the axons becoming myelinated, or insulated. Axons (the part of the neuron that transmits impulses away from the cell body) become sheathed in myelin that protects and insulates them, allowing messages to move faster and more efficiently from one neuron to another. The more the pathway is used, the greater the insulation, or myelination, of the axon, which results in higher efficiency and speed in message delivery.

Imagine the brain as a computer that has an electrical cord running to it. The neurons create pathways that operate like the cord that carries electricity from the wall outlet to the computer. The myelination is like the rubber insulation around the cord; the insulation improves the speed and efficiency of the message.

As the brain becomes more automatized, new pathways are established, increasing the functionality of the brain. This is like connecting the computer to a printer, or an external hard drive, or a scanner. When you plug in these peripheral devices, via a cord that runs from the device to the computer, you are adding functionality to the computer; the more devices that are connected to the computer, the more options or resources the computer has available to it. That is the same principal as interconnectivity, which makes it possible for a child to draw from different neurological resources related to the same task. The more options, the greater the interconnectivity. As interconnectivity increases, we increase the capacity to see things from different points of view, and thus our ability to handle change or unpredictability increases.

NEURON COMMUNICATION

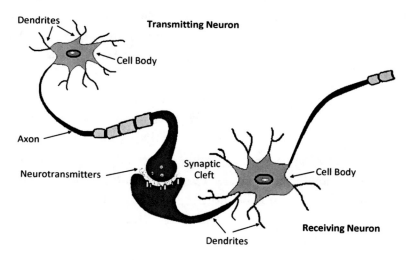

Diagram 4.1 - The distinct structure of neurons make them well suited to their specialized role of information processing and communication.

Neurological interconnectivity impacts flexibility, executive functioning, and processing of everything except the most finite, black and white data. The lack of interconnectivity is what causes the thinking of someone on the spectrum to seem rigid and compartmentalized.

Sensory Perception and Social Development

We do not need to be taught to take in the sensory environment; it is automatic. When we absorb sensory information, we do so without putting a great deal of effort into the action; our body learns to do this automatically. In other words, it does not require conscious thought to perform.

From birth, our perceptions are forced upon us as we age, just by our existence in the physical world. These sensory perceptions are what stimulate our brains to begin to develop, perceive, and organize our surroundings neurologically. We cannot help but take this information in and make sense of it while we process it, altering our sense of self and our sense of self as it pertains to the world around us. We are forced via development to do so.

In a neuro-typical child, early childhood is an amazing time for neurological development. Throughout the first few months and years of life, all of the brain's energy is devoted to this task. The child quickly begins to perceive social interactions, chiefly with her primary caregiver, typically her mother. She recognizes mom's voice, smell, face, and mannerisms very early in development.

As part of this sensory perception process, social development also begins to occur automatically for neuro-typical kids. For example, when my youngest daughter was 5, she was watching the kids in the neighborhood playing a game called four square in our driveway while waiting for the bus to take them to school. Cece was not playing; she was standing off to the side watching and listening to everything that was going on during the game. When the other kids laughed at something, Cece laughed. She is one of the youngest in the neighborhood, and was learning to be social by watching the older kids play.

The key concept to understand is that I did not tell her to pay attention to the other kids in the driveway; she was motivated to pay attention to them by her innate desire to grow socially. The more she watched the other children, the more automatized her social understanding became. Did I teach her that? No. As human beings, we are hardwired to do this. The process of high-level social development was happening in her brain automatically as she took in and made sense of the interactions between the other kids. Neuro-typical kids naturally learn to be social by watching people behave socially. Not so with a child on the spectrum.

Social development does not come automatically for the child with autism spectrum disorder. These kids can be so deeply overwhelmed with other stimuli that the nuances of social interaction aren't easily visible to them. They may be so intensely involved with processing physical sensory stimuli that their systems are working full force to cope with input that most neuro-typical people wouldn't even notice. Such stimuli might be the brightness of the light outside, the heat of the day, or something totally imperceptible to most of us, like the feel of socks on their feet. Imagine when you have something stuck in your teeth and you just can't get it free; that can require a great deal of mental energy to process and can be very distracting. That is similar to the way autistic processing saps the individual's ability to process other input, especially social.

ALLOCATION OF RESOURCES/AUTOMATIZING TASKS

Imagine the human brain as a 9-volt battery. In the entire lifetime of the individual, the brain does not increase in available energy; it is always a 9-volt battery. As such, it has a specific, limited amount of energy resources inherent to it. In order to accomplish more tasks (e.g., learning to walk, talk, read, etc.), the battery would either need to get larger (which it can't) or become more efficient at accomplishing the same tasks by utilizing less energy, thus allowing the re-allocation of the now-unneeded resources for another task.

The human brain uses its finite resources to process information in a hierarchical system—from lower level information (concrete) to higher level (more abstract)—in order to learn, self-organize, and become efficient. During normal development, tasks that the brain has become efficient in performing are called automatized, which means that these tasks happen automatically without a great deal of cognitive focus.

The more efficient the brain becomes in processing and organizing one's experiences, the greater the number of tasks that become automatized, resulting in more energy being freed up for higher level processing. Our brains cannot acquire more energy; instead they are designed to become efficient with the energy they have, freeing up resources for other tasks.

Imagine a child learning to walk. As the child's neurological system is self-organizing (i.e., learning to make coordinated movements using the balance system and the visual system in such a manner as to move the body forward in an upright fashion), all the brain's resources are allocated to this task. If you distract a baby when he is first learning to walk, he will lose his balance and fall over. The act of walking has not yet become an automatized function; the action requires conscious thought (more resources) in order for the baby to do it. Once the neurological interconnectivity is established for the action of walking (walking becomes automatized), the individual is able to walk and perform other tasks at the same time.

As adults, we also experience the process of allocation of resources and automatization as we learn new tasks. Think about learning to drive. Was this an automatized function for you when you were 16 years old taking driver's education class? It was not. You were unable to drive a car with distractions present. Once the action of operating a car became automatized, it did not require the same effort or energy to perform. You can now drive, adjust the radio, and talk on your cell phone all at the same time (although that's not recommended!).

Due to its energy capacity limit, the human brain must allocate resources. When a function is not automatized, a great deal of the brain's resources must be allocated to accomplish the task. The more automatic any function becomes, the more efficient the brain becomes, and the less energy it uses on the task. Thus, the brain is an energy transformation system, streamlining processes and conserving neurological energy as it incorporates new information, skills, and experiences neurologically. This process also builds interconnectivity.

Resource allocation is different in kids on the spectrum. Tasks that are easily accomplished by other kids may require a great deal more resources for a child on the spectrum. Remember the example of a younger child learning social nuances by watching older kids play the four square game? In that same situation, a child on the spectrum might be using all of her resources to cope with the feel of the shoes she has just put on to go outside, the sensation of the jacket on her back, the sound of the ball bouncing, or the smell of the grass that has just been mowed. As a result, she may not even notice the four square game. Unable to even see the game, it is a near impossibility that she will receive and process the higher level social information.

A child with ASD simply can't process all that input at one time; his neurological system proceeds to process input in a hierarchical order, from the more basic physical stimuli up to the most complicated social interaction. Interpersonal communication is one of the highest levels of processing the human brain undertakes. If this child's neurological resources are consumed with the basics, there's nothing available to process higher level input, i.e., social information. That's why social interactions are difficult for a child on the spectrum.

ASSOCIATIVE AND COGNITIVE TASKS

Another way to look at the allocation of resources is in terms of whether a task is *cognitive* or *associative*. A cognitive task is one that requires all the brain's effort and thought to execute. The act of learning to walk or learning to drive a car would be examples of cognitive tasks. At first, all of our conscious thought needs to be allocated to the new task that we are trying to accomplish. Eventually, once we master that task, it becomes an associative task that we can perform simultaneously with other tasks. For example, driving is an associative task for most of us; we can drive, talk, sing, and eat all at the same time.

But it isn't always that way. When I first sat behind the wheel to drive a stick shift car, it required all my energy. One time, I didn't hit the clutch quickly enough and the car stalled. I had trouble operating both the clutch and the stick at the same time. It was hard to coordinate releasing my foot off the clutch, pressing the gas pedal, watching where I was going, and steering simultaneously. Now, I can do all of the aforementioned tasks while I adjust my radio or dial or plug in a CD. Working a clutch and driving a stick shift has gone from being a cognitive task to an associative task for me.

Today, if I am driving and all three of my girls are in my truck, and the music is playing, and we are laughing, and the road starts to get icy, what happens? The task goes from an associative task back to a cognitive task. What do I say to my kids? I say, "Children, what was an associative task is now a cognitive task." Just kidding. In these situations, I do tell them to keep the noise down because my focus must be on driving. Almost everything we learn starts as a cognitive task and then, more than likely, becomes an associative task.

I remember as a graduate student driving home on the Interstate from Chicago to the suburbs late at night and taking the exit ramp to my house without even realizing what I was doing. I had performed this action so many times that I automatically took the exit without conscious thought. Driving home had become an associative task for me.

Learning to play a musical instrument is a good example of a task that develops from cognitive to associative. The first time you play an instrument, you need to think about, and put conscious effort into, every aspect of playing. Eventually, you can play the instrument easily, without tremendous cognitive effort.

Another good example is sports. Think about a professional quarterback when he is throwing a football during a game on a Sunday afternoon. The act of throwing the football for him is very automatic. He is able to process the play, the defense, and the snap count, determine if a blitz is coming, run to his left and throw back across the field, and hit a moving target in stride. While he is doing all this, he is not thinking about throwing the football. The act of throwing has become automatized—it does not require conscious thought and effort on his part. Through his hard, concentrated, motivated effort, he has developed a neurological architecture that enables him to throw a football automatically, the same way you learned to walk, drive a car, or play a musical instrument.

Walking and talking are associative tasks. We can do both at the same time. The act of walking and the development of the muscles needed to walk require a lot of energy and concentrated effort to perform (that's where the phrase, "You can't walk and chew gum" comes from.) As we learn to perform different tasks, we become neurologically efficient and the tasks require less of our brains' available energy, thus those tasks become automatized, or associative, tasks. This is normal neurological development. For children with ASD, allocating energy resources and processing the environment are much different and may never become automatized as they would for a neuro-typical individual.

PROCESSING THE SOCIAL ENVIRONMENT

Socializing works in a similar way to learning new tasks; the more efficient we become, the less energy we use to engage in social activity. As a neuro-typical child develops, processing the environment becomes an associative task; lower level neurological systems and social processing become more automatized. Again, this is different for children on the spectrum, who can't effectively process all the stimuli simultaneously.

Understanding the difference in the level of automatization of the social environment for people with ASD is a key factor to interpreting their behavior. As parents and educators, we often mistakenly assume that many of the tasks that are associative for most people (i.e., looking at someone and listening to him at the same time) will also be associative for children with autism—that may be totally false. Those same functions could each be cognitive for individuals on the spectrum. Many individuals on the spectrum have trouble with eye contact and/or cannot process visual and auditory information at the same time. My clients often ask me, "Would you like me to listen to you or look at you?" I tell them to listen to what I am saying. Parents and teachers often say to a child, "Look at me when I'm talking to you." This can be overloading to kids on the spectrum. Looking at the teacher (i.e., processing visual stimulus) is a cognitive task.

Imagine the frustration and confusion of a fourth grade student with ASD who tried to pay attention to his teacher by looking at her. The more he focused on watching her, the harder it was for him to listen to what she was saying to him. He was unable to effectively understand her words at the same time he was watching her. He came home from school very frustrated; he was unable to comprehend why he couldn't understand the teacher like the other kids, especially when he tried so hard to pay attention. As a result, his anxiety level soared.

I have worked with a lot of kids whose teachers had sent them to the office for not listening. In reality, they were only perceived as not listening because they were not looking at the teacher. In the case of that fourth grade boy, he did look at the teacher, but as a result, he was unable to hear what she was saying. Due to the neurological overload, these kids can't process what the teacher is saying if they are looking at her! This will become even easier to understand as the neurological development for those on the autism spectrum is explained.

HOMEOSTASIS AND HABITUATION

Human beings are hardwired so that when sensory stimulation enters our receptive fields, our bodies react. For example, when you put clothes on this morning, you were adding new sensory stimulation to your receptive field (your skin).

Whenever new stimuli are received, the brain evaluates that stimulation and determines if it is dangerous (e.g., a hot stove) or overbearing (a wool sweater in summer); and then, if not, the brain processes the stimulation to return to a sense of calm, or *homeostasis*.

The body starts at homeostasis; stimulation enters the receptive field and excitatory neurons fire. When the stimulation reaches a certain threshold, the brain evaluates the information and decides that it is not life threatening, so it activates the inhibitory neurons, which brings the body back to homeostasis and a sense of calm. Homeostasis is the body's way of continually adjusting to maintain a sense of calm on a neurological level. In other words, we get used to, or *habituate*, the feeling of wearing clothes, and it is no longer part of our conscious awareness. The process of adapting to any stimulation is called *habituation*, and the body does this all day long with every sensory channel (see Diagram 4.2).

When getting dressed, you probably noticed the way the fabric felt on your skin when you first put on your clothes, then forgot about it. The outfit you put on this morning is still touching your skin, but your body is no longer reacting to the stimulus of the clothes contacting it; your body is calm on a neurological level. Therefore, you are not consciously aware of the feeling of your clothes unless you focus on them. What if the body was unable to inhibit the feelings of the shirt or pants? The body would then be in a constant state of excitation. This could very well be the case for individuals with ASD.

While reading this book, can you hear noises in the room? Try it. Everybody can, if you think about it. Are you having trouble tuning out that stimulation in order to read? Your brain tells itself that the

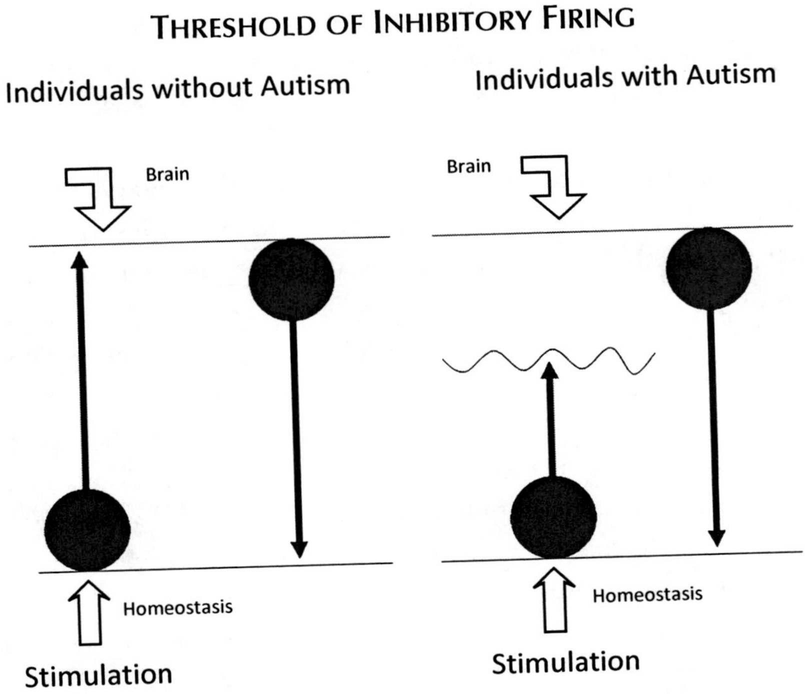
THRESHOLD OF INHIBITORY FIRING
Individuals without Autism
Individuals with Autism
Brain
Brain
Homeostasis
Homeostasis
Stimulation
Stimulation

Diagram 4.2 -This diagram illustrates how the neuro-typical brain responds to stimuli (left side). In the autistic brain, the signal gets stuck before the brain can process what the signal is and it creates chaos.

stimulation in the room is irrelevant and you habituate to it, allowing yourself to read and process the words on the page. Now, of course, you are going to think about it because I brought it up, but until that point, you habituated to the sounds in the room. Consider, for a moment, people who can sleep in downtown Chicago while the L-train is going by their apartments. You think, "There is no way I could do that!" But, if you lived there long enough, you could; you would adjust to the noise by habituation—unless you had a heightened sensory system.

It is possible that incoming stimulation can be too much for the system to handle and calm itself down. If you are at a rock 'n roll concert, you will not be able to tune out the extremely loud sound of the music. What if you were surrounded by blaring rock music 24/7? How hard would it be to process the environment if your body was in that type of constant state of excitation and you could never get back to homeostasis? Talk about anxiety!

Let's look at kids on the spectrum. They put their clothes on in the morning. What happens if the excitatory neurons fire, but they don't reach the threshold that activates the inhibitory neurons needed to calm themselves down and habituate to the environment (see Diagram 4.2)? The impulse (or signal) gets stuck here. Now, the neurons do not habituate; they are in this constant state of excitation.

Children in this dilemma have two options: 1) take their clothes off to remove the stimulation; or 2) try to deal with the stimulation. If they cannot remove the stimulation, they have a bit of a quandary. So, what do they do to deal with stimulation that they cannot naturally tune out the way neuro-typical children can? They develop behaviors to cope. Now, we see some of the autistic tendencies, for example, removing clothing, rocking, chewing, or hyperfocusing, etc. These behaviors close the sensory gap, remove, or tune out the stimulation and thus allow the body to return to homeostasis.

What these children are actually doing is providing their bodies with more stimulation. More stimulation leads to the activation of the excitatory neurons, which brings them closer to the threshold that allows the brain to activate the inhibitory neurons, which, in turn, calms them and allows them to habituate to the environment. The bridging of this gap is often referred to as a *sensory break*. Sensory breaks are so important to children on the spectrum. Their bodies require additional sensory stimulation to help them self-regulate, i.e., return to homeostasis or habituate to the stimuli surrounding them, and thus become calm. Although this is an automatic process in individuals without autism, it may not be automatic in those with autism.

In Diagram 4.2, the left side represents what should be happening normally on a neurological level; the right side represents the brain activity of someone with ASD. Even though children on the spectrum are thought to be hypersensitive to the environment, they still don't seem to reach the neurological threshold that allows their bodies to return to homeostasis. That leads to some, if not all, of the challenges associated with autism.

The excitatory/inhibitory neuron discussion may also help to explain the treatment used for individuals with attention deficit disorder (ADD) and attention deficit hyperactive disorder (ADHD). These individuals also appear to be in a constant state of excitation. While it may appear counter-intuitive, giving them a stimulant (such as Ritalin) seems to boost the excitatory neurons to a level that activates the firing of inhibitory neurons, resulting in a return to a calm state.

A key part of any treatment, either at a doctor's office, at home, or in school, is to figure out what is needed for each child to help him regulate and calm his body down in terms of the sensory environment. Therapy is ineffective if the child is stuck in a constant state of excitation. I bet there have been 10,000 jumping jacks done in my office. I ask the kids to do them to further stimulate their excitatory neurons in an effort to help calm them down. In the 1980s, mini trampolines became popular for working out. Now, this is a tool for kids with sensory regulation issues! Kids can jump up and down on this little trampoline to help calm themselves. The amount of time spent jumping on the trampoline, or doing jumping jacks, is directly related to the amount of stimulation the individual requires, and that depends on the child. If a child does not get enough of the trampoline, he may actually be more wound up than when he started. (For further discussion about this, refer to Chapter 15, Treatments and Techniques.)

Temple Grandin is one of the country's leading experts on autism. She is an international speaker and teacher, and has autism herself. She has developed a "squeeze machine," which she uses to apply sensory stimulation to her body in order to help her calm down when she is overwhelmed. This machine applies pressure to her body, bridging the sensory gap, which allows her to return to a calm state. The machine actually applies proprioceptive stimulation. Proprioception is the sense of the orientation of one's limbs in space—this is the brain's mechanism that keeps you from running into a door jamb or makes it possible for you to slap a mosquito on your back without being able to see it. The technique of adding stimulation to cause the brain to reach the threshold of inhibitory firing could apply for any type of sensory stimulation, not just tactile. As I've already mentioned, some common stimulating behaviors seen in people with autism include repetitive actions like flapping, rocking, spinning, or chewing.

The important point is that stimulus created by autistic behavior has two purposes: 1) to bridge the sensory gap in the brain, which then allows the body to return to homeostasis; and 2) to be used as a distraction to block out the painful or confusing environment.

We can teach kids to recognize when they are stuck short of the stimulation they need to return to homeostasis. In other words, teach them to recognize when they are at the point where they want to engage in behavior that is stimulating. As is often the case, the behavior of choice may not be socially acceptable, so managing this behavior is an important aspect of therapy. In order to be functional, we all need to fit in to some degree. So, learning not to publicly display socially questionable behavior reduces the friction in the child's life.

You can teach a child to recognize when his body needs to be calmed down and you can teach him how to do that in a socially acceptable way. In therapy, I teach kids to be proactive, to recognize when they are overwhelmed by the environment, and to learn what they can do in order to calm themselves down. This is discussed in detail in the chapters on treatment options.

It is very possible for higher functioning individuals to manage themselves so that the stimming behavior that had occurred all the time, or in public places, or in situations that might make the person appear odd, now only occurs once per day, at home, in private. I work with one young man who has been able to accomplish just that.

When I first met him, he engaged in self-stimulatory behavior during his entire school day. He would flap his hands when he was nervous or upset. We worked on scheduling the times he would self-stimulate during his day and he made an effort to do so in private. We also adapted some other fidgets he could use for his hands when he really felt like stimming. Eventually, he was able to stim in the morning before school, twice during school, after school, and then before bed. In addition, we eliminated the stimming at school (by using an object in his hands like a coin, a rubber ball, or a key chain). Finally, he was able to control the flapping behavior, engaging in it only before bedtime. Today, he successfully manages his state, and you will not see any of his stimming behavior.

CHAPTER 5

STAGES OF NORMAL CHILD DEVELOPMENT

The more flexible we become, the more we are able to handle unpredictability. The opposite dynamic occurs in individuals with ASD as their minds strive to reduce unpredictability and to create sameness.

To truly understand the impact of the autistic neurological architecture, it is important to have some knowledge of the stages of normal child development. In comparison to what is typical, the differences in the autistic development make more sense. Remember, autistic behavioral differences are neurologically based.

Following is a brief description of the stages of normal neurological child development (see the chart below). The key concept to grasp as it relates to understanding ASD is that each of the stages of normal development includes social aspects, which occur automatically as part of development in a neuro-typical child. We do not teach the ability to read social nuances in the classroom although we teach rules, expectations, courtesy, etc. In neuro-typical individuals, that social component comes naturally as part of our human hardwiring.

Human beings are intrinsically motivated to interact socially; it is part of the human psyche to be social beings. Given normal functioning, developing socially is our brain's default programming—it will happen automatically.

CHILD DEVELOPMENT CHART

Stage	Age	Neurological Development
Engagement	Birth-8 months	Differentiation
Two Way Communication	18 months	Interconnectivity Develops
Shared Meaning	18-36 months	Interconnectivity Develops
Emotional Thinking	Ages 3, 4, 5	Interconnectivity Develops
Social Comparison	Begins about age 3	Minor Neurons Develop
Neurological Flexibility	As early as 3-4	Active Interconnectivity

ENGAGEMENT

As I've mentioned in Chapter 4, How Autism Develops, when we enter the world as newborns, we immediately begin to process the sensory environment. An interesting dynamic takes place as we process this new world surrounding us. We learn to navigate the sensory environment both physically, with our neurological systems, and socially, through a process called *engagement*, usually with the help of our primary caregiver. A newborn begins the process of engagement instantly after birth and typically continues until about 8 months old.

Physically, a baby enters the world relatively intact. For example, a child's visual system is able to perceive stimuli up to about seven inches. She can also hear, smell, taste, and feel the environment.

Mother and father engage with their child by responding to her needs. When the baby cries, they pick her up, change her, feed her, rock her, etc. The baby learns that when she feels any discomfort and she performs this social act (crying), an amazing thing happens—comforted by another human being, she begins to feel better and she stops crying. This is obviously not always the case, but, for the most part, the child is soothed when her parents act to comfort her.

Babies begin to become more social as they continue to develop; we make funny faces at them, or make noises to engage with them. We stick out our tongues and the baby sticks out his tongue. Mothers coo and talk with their babies (this is called *motherese*). A mother is often able to recognize her child's needs based on the type of cry or the level of distress the child exhibits. This is the social process of engagement. The more the child engages, the more the brain's neurons differentiate themselves to the social interaction.

Many children who spend time in orphanages after birth are not given the opportunity to engage with people, and this, in turn, has a severe impact on their ability to form bonds and relationships. Unfortunately, these children are often significantly impaired and are diagnosed with reactive attachment disorder. What their body craves neurologically is not available to them, and they are basically starved of the social process of engagement. Thus, the interconnectivity in their neurons is restricted, creating long-term difficulty with interpersonal interaction.

This is different than what happens in a child with ASD, whose neurological predisposition does not create the craving for the social process. Children with autism can still be extroverted, but their sensory challenges impede their ability to process the environment and thereby impede their understanding of the subtleties (such as nonverbal behaviors) of social development.

TWO-WAY COMMUNICATION

What's the first word a child learns that demonstrates communication? *No.* "Pick that up." "No." "Time for bed." "No." This is two-way communication, the beginning of a child demonstrating his ability to communicate with other individuals. At this stage, children begin to learn the social practice of communicating a want, a need, or a feeling. This is not something we have to teach them. They are hardwired to learn it.

Two-way communication is not always verbal. When her older sisters would be watching TV, my youngest daughter would take the remote control and shut it off—*when she was 13 months old.* She was looking for attention when her sisters were watching TV, so she would turn it off, causing frustration for her sisters. Sometimes, I would be watching a football game and, of course, it would be 4th and goal, last play of the game, and I would hear that sound a TV makes just before it shuts off, then a little giggle and feet slapping on the tile as the TV went blank, and there would go Cece, running down the hallway with the remote. Trust me, I did not teach her how to turn off the TV. The point I want to emphasize is that this was not something anyone in our household taught her. So, how did she learn to do that? She learned by paying attention to the environment, taking it in, processing it, and having a desire to communicate. She figures out that the little red button on the remote turns off the TV, and makes the connection, "I want my dad's attention" and *click!* That's two-way communication, and it is socially driven.

Language development is motivated by a desire to be social. As we learn to communicate, through both our words and actions, we increase our ability to engage with others and to get our basic biological and emotional wants and needs met. The same daughter who turned off the TV at 13 months old was not highly motivated to learn to talk because she had two older sisters who would talk for her. When I said, "Cece, say please," she would just sit there and her sisters would say it for her. When her sisters asked her to say please, sure enough, Cece would say please. Her desire to communicate was socially based. She would communicate with her parents only to please her sisters. This probably wouldn't happen with a child with autism, who might not communicate at all.

SHARED MEANING

As a child moves farther along the continuum of normal development, she begins to develop her ability to communicate meaning, to qualify how she is feeling. At this stage, children will expand the simple "No" by saying, "I don't have to," or "You can't make me," or "You are not the boss of me," etc. This is when children develop the ability to quantify reasons behind their actions. Shared meaning is characterized by an increase in the amount of information that is relayed.

EMOTIONAL THINKING

As a child continues to grow, he starts to develop emotional understanding and emotional thinking. Emotional thinking is unique; it begins to create social understanding at a much higher level. An individual's thinking shifts from, "it's all about me" to a broader awareness and understanding about the people around him. For example, ask a 3 to 5-year-old to identify the smart kids in his class or neighborhood, and he usually has the answer. Ask the same kid about the not-so-smart kids in the neighborhood, and he will know that, too. Is this ability to intuitively know who is smart and who is not a result of nature or training? Do we teach kids this on purpose? Do parents or educators go out into the neighborhood with the children and point out the smart kids and the not-so-smart kids? Do they sit the kindergartners down and say, "Today, we are going to learn how to pick out the smart kids in the class"? Of course not, yet this ability to identify differences in others clearly begins to develop in neurologically normal kids.

So, how does this skill develop? During the emotional thinking stage of development, kids begin to *self-organize,* that is the ability to learn how they fit in and how they interact—they learn as they watch what others are doing. Self-organization helps neuro-typical children learn to regulate and process the social environment; they watch on a conscious level, but they are not aware that they are learning this social skill of fitting in. Kids are motivated to self-organize by their instinctive desire to grow socially (a desire that usually is not present in kids with ASD or, if it is present, it is compromised by their sensory challenges). Emotional thinking is a remarkable phenomenon. It is incredible to watch how kids naturally develop social understanding through self-organizing.

For example, the little boy next door, Christian, is the oldest kid in my neighborhood. One day, I was watching from a distance while this scenario unfolded: eight kids wanted to sit on the hammock in the back yard, but, of course, they did not all fit. I could see the kids listening to Christian as he told them who would get on the hammock and who would push. That is self-organizing; the kids were automatically responding to the social environment and the social hierarchy. Children do it entirely on their own, as an outgrowth of their neurological hardwiring. I did not teach it, and they do not need guidance to do it effectively.

During the emotional thinking phase, as children begin to watch and analyze what other children are doing around them, they begin to compare themselves to others. This is how they begin to learn social behavior. This also gives rise to the development of an interesting group of neurons called *mirror neurons.*

Mirror neurons allow us to learn vicariously, by witnessing the experiences of others. These neurons, located throughout our brains, allow us to learn by watching, and to feel what others around us are feeling without actually experiencing what they have gone through. In other words, we can watch someone perform a task and learn to perform the task ourselves just by watching. We can also instinctively know how someone might feel in a given situation or circumstance. When you grimace and think, "Oh, that must really hurt" because you have seen someone else smash their hand with a hammer, you are reacting to the information that is being processed by your mirror neurons. This is what enables us to watch a movie and feel sad about what is going on in the movie even though we are not in the movie or personally experiencing the situation.

Have you ever fed a baby? When you hold up the spoon, her mouth opens, so you start moving your mouth the same way the baby does. These are mirror neurons at work. As our mirror neurons develop, so does our ability to develop empathy and our ability to feel for other people. Remember, in neuro-typical individuals, these skills develop naturally and without instruction, and, as they develop, they strengthen neurological interconnectivity in the brain.

SOCIAL COMPARISON

The development of emotional thinking prepares us for the next step in social growth, which is *social comparison*. Social comparison is exactly what the name implies; we compare ourselves to others. This really begins at around age 3, and it is part of what makes it possible for kids to tell us who the smart kids are in the neighborhood, even though we don't teach them that skill. Neuro-typical children figure it out on their own because human beings are hardwired and innately motivated to be social. This process of social comparison takes place whether we like it or not. The most important thing to know about social comparison is that, for a neuro-typical individual, it is an automatic process. It starts when children are very young and it happens automatically.

One of the best selling papers in the world is *The National Enquirer*. Why is that? Because people want to know what Brad and Angie are doing, whether they want to adopt another baby, or if they are fighting over Jennifer. That is social comparison. We cannot help but do that; in our culture, it is addictive. Keeping up with the Joneses is driven by social comparison.

Can you imagine what it would be like to never worry about comparing ourselves to others? To not care about how we look, how we smell, or how we act, etc.? As humans, we cannot avoid comparing ourselves to others because we live in a social society and our ability to function is dependent on getting along with other people and fitting in on some level. How many people go to work and forget to comb their hair? (I have actually done that—my excuse is that I was a busy graduate student at the time and did not realize it until someone at work asked me what was up with my hair.) This type of behavior does not happen very often because we don't want to embarrass ourselves. We want to wear what everybody else is wearing, fit in with the latest styles, and basically not appear different from others. I am not saying that we do not want to be individuals and walk to the beat of our own drum, but we still strive to comply with social norms and expectations to some degree in order to survive and function in society. Due to the nature of their difficulties, this can be hard for people with ASD.

When she was 5 years old, my oldest daughter asked me if I would stop giving her a kiss at the bus stop. I agreed, but asked why. She told me that it was because I was the only dad at the bus stop. I asked her if anyone had said anything to her about the fact that I was the only dad at the bus stop or the fact that I gave her a kiss before she got on the bus. Guess what she said? "No." No one had said anything to her or made any comments, but she was comparing herself to the other children at the bus stop and she did not want to appear different or risk being teased. At age 5, she was already very socially aware and she was taking steps to make sure that she did not appear different than other children.

Comparing one's self to others peaks in middle school, typically grades 6, 7, and 8, as children are going through puberty and developing autonomy, or a sense of self. At that age, they are really striving to be cool and fit in, to be like everybody else, as well as to figure out who they are as individuals.

Years ago, I read a research article that described social comparison; it included a picture showing about eight middle school girls standing in front of a large mirror in the school bathroom. Can you guess what they were all looking at? Maybe their hair? Or, their make-up? Nope—they were looking at each other.

One day, my oldest daughter and I were watching the national spelling bee on ESPN. One contestant (who ended up winning) stepped up to the microphone when it was her turn. She went through the same process as everyone else: definition, pronunciation, word origin, etc. It took her some time to begin to spell the word. She finally said, "B" and then took a step back and began flapping her arms and hands like a bird. Elli could not believe what she was seeing! "Dad, what is she doing? Doesn't she know people are watching?" I could see the beads of sweat forming on Elli's forehead and the anxiety she felt watching this young lady on stage. She could not believe that this girl would do this in front of everyone. Elli is very socially aware, to the point of creating some anxiety about doing the right thing or fitting in.

Social comparison affects the functional world of adults every day. I grew up in North Dakota, where there is basically no traffic. Ten cars at a stoplight was our idea of a busy intersection. When I first moved to Illinois to attend graduate school in Chicago, I drove into the city from the suburbs every day. I really had trouble getting a handle on this whole traffic thing, rush hour, etc. How could I be on a major road and be at a dead standstill? Then one day, I heard the radio announcer say that there was a "gaper's delay" causing a backup on the toll road. I remember wondering, "What could a gaper's delay be?" The only thing I could imagine was that it must be a truck that broke down or had an accident, a "gaper truck."

Later, I learned that it was a delay caused by people watching what is happening on the side of the road. In some parts of the country, this phenomenon is referred to as "rubber-necking." It could be the result of an accident or someone changing a flat tire. Not only does it slow down the traffic that is traveling in the same direction, but it also slows traffic traveling in the opposite direction! When I heard this, I remember thinking, "How can someone changing a tire slow traffic down to a halt in both directions?" Gaper's delays demonstrate social comparison. People driving by the incident think, "I have to see what is going on, is it a bad accident, any blood?" More accidents are caused because of this. The irony is that most people do not stop to help; they just really want to see what is going on. Our lives are impacted by social comparison all the time.

In general, social interaction is one of the most complex things we do; it is never the same twice. The players change, the situations change, the timing changes. There are no two identical social situations. So, as we engage and interact, we learn to adapt and to be flexible, adjusting to the subtle changes in our interactions. Social comparison is part of the process.

Something very interesting begins to take place as we participate in these complicated social interactions and compare ourselves to others. The more we do it, the more we strengthen the neurological interconnectivity in our brain and, as a result, we learn to be flexible. We learn that every interaction and experience differs, even if only slightly. We learn to adapt to the abstract nature of the social interaction. By virtue of experiencing this constant change, neurological interconnectivity increases in our brain, and this results in more flexibility.

NEUROLOGICAL FLEXIBILITY

As the brain develops and social interaction becomes more automatized, the brain establishes faster, more efficient neural pathways, allowing the neurons to communicate more and more efficiently. Thus, we become better suited to handle change and unpredictability. The more interconnectivity among neurons in the brain, the more we can see things from different angles, or handle situations that are slightly different from anything that we have experienced before. We become more flexible.

The more flexible we become, the more we are able to handle unpredictability. For example, if I am driving to work in the morning, and I know there is construction on my way, I might decide to take another route. On this route, I encounter more construction. I did not plan on it, but I will adapt to it and be okay with it; I can be flexible. I will not get upset because I am able to change my route. That's what starts to happen as we engage socially, we adapt. Being social is not a static or linear function; it is dynamic, always changing, always different.

Ultimately, the entire process of normal child development builds experience, skill, and flexibility leading up to a point when the child can effectively navigate in an abstract social world. The flexibility that develops is a result of the interconnectivity on a neurological level, which lays the foundation for the behavior of the individual. The opposite dynamic occurs in individuals with ASD as their minds strive to reduce unpredictability and to create sameness.

CHAPTER 6

SPECTRUM DEVELOPMENT

An individual with autism has a processing system that can be described as a nonflexible, static linear approach. This is not meant as a value judgment; this type of processing is not wrong—it's just different.

*N*ow that you have some background in normal child development, you can begin to understand how development is different for those with ASD and why their perceptions seem different from those previously described. Children on the spectrum develop a very different way of navigating and processing the world around them compared to their neuro-typical brothers and sisters. This is an outgrowth of the shared common characteristic of individuals with ASD—their neurological difficulty in processing and making sense of the incoming sensory information. As a result, they struggle with sensory hypersensitivity, becoming controlling and rigid. They develop linear, black and white thinking. These issues impact their communication, social development, and executive functioning, which is the ability to project oneself into the future and make connections between results and actions.

SENSORY HYPERSENSITIVITY: THE TIMES 10 FACTOR

One of the primary features of individuals with ASD is their apparent hypersensitivity to the sensory environment, through any of the sensory channels (hearing, touch, taste, etc.), if not most or all of them. The onset of overabundance, or overload, of sensory information entering the receptive field of a child on the spectrum begins very early in life. Incoming information, for whatever reason, seems to be turned up a few notches for these children; it is as if their dials are turned up 10 times that of individuals without ASD.

Some theories argue that children on the spectrum are hypersensitive (oversensitive) to the environment and some argue that they are hyposensitive (under responsive). In my opinion, much of what is perceived as hyposensitivity can be attributed to children on the spectrum tuning out the environment that is not making sense. I recently evaluated a child on the spectrum whose parents told me that they originally thought their child was deaf. They reported to me seeing him sitting on the floor in the kitchen stimming with a toy; they would call his name and he would not respond. They even tried to bang pots and pans together behind their son—he did not even flinch. They took him for a hearing evaluation because they thought that he must have a hearing impairment. Ultimately, they found out that his hearing was well within the normal range. It was as if their son could turn his hearing off. He could focus so intently on the object he was stimming on that he could tune out other sensory input entirely.

Current research suggests that individuals on the spectrum do not have any physiological difference in their sensory receptors, which means, for example, that their hearing is not impaired. However, when the sensory information reaches the brain it is magnified or scrambled in some way. In some cases, all the sensory information seems to enter at once and the brain is unable to filter out irrelevant information. This can be true for any of the sensory channels.

For example, children with autism often have tactile sensitivities; they dislike being touched. It seems to be very common for these individuals to have a dislike of new clothing, particularly socks with the sewing line in the toes. They may also find it difficult to tolerate a change in seasonal clothing, for instance, when they switch from short sleeves in the summer to long sleeves in fall. They tend to dislike belts, tags in their shirts, or the feel of certain fabrics. Many toddlers would rather be naked than wear diapers; even middle school kids prefer to take off their clothes when they are at home. The rule of thumb that I use to help people understand the experience of those on the spectrum is that they have 10 times the sensory experience of the average neuro-typical individual and, therefore, they deal with a lot of discomfort and sensitivity.

Many children on the autistic spectrum are also very picky about food, and will only eat and drink a very limited number of items. Nearly three-quarters of the clients I see demand Chicken McNuggets™ from MacDonald's. There could be a variety of reasons why individuals with ASD who have gastrointestinal sensory issues only want to eat certain foods. The texture of the food could be part of the problem. Kids with autism may not be able to tolerate slimy, crunchy, or sloppy foods. What do individuals without ASD do if a certain food bothers their stomachs? They avoid it! What if you were not sure what foods were going to bother your stomach? Would you be apt to try all sorts of different foods, or would you stick to a very strict diet? Now imagine your stomach pain and multiply it by 10. Avoiding foods that bother you would now become a flat out refusal to touch them. In many cases, if an individual with ASD has a negative experience with certain foods, he will not want to try other new foods because of the fear of the pain they may cause.

Sensitivity to loud sounds is also common; many of these kids can't stand to be in crowded places. Sometimes, noise sensitivity can be related to frequency rather than volume. When the child has a sensitivity to noise, you will see her covering her ears to muffle loud or odd noises.

This sensory times 10 overreaction often happens when toilet training children with ASD; problems using the bathroom, such as pain, toilet flushing, or slow toilet training, etc., often occur and are usually sensory-related issues. If they have one negative experience with a bowel movement, they try and hold it to avoid the pain in the future. This, however, just compounds the problem.

Physical discomfort is very distracting. Imagine that you have the flu and you try to work and conduct yourself in a professional and productive manner. You tell yourself that you are not going to let the fact that your stomach hurts impact your day in any way. Are you able to do that, or is it very hard to be productive and not let your stomach bother you? Or, do you spend a great deal of your day thinking about your symptoms? Imagine if every day were so uncomfortable and you were required to rise above it to function. That's what it may feel like to those on the spectrum. It would be 10 times harder if you had to do it everyday.

Any sensory problem a child on the spectrum experiences is further exacerbated by the fact that these individuals typically have difficulty communicating what is bothering them. They resort to primitive ways of controlling the environment so as to avoid what is painful or disturbing to them.

Thus, the behavioral manifestations of ASD appear. Rocking, spinning the wheels of a toy car, staring into space or zoning out, throwing extreme tantrums with the slightest change in the environment, lining up objects, hyperfocusing on an object such as a calendar or a clock, and/or spending time in the corner away from others are just some of the behaviors that develop as a result of children with ASD trying to manage their neurological sensitivity issues. These children are sometimes even described as aloof or withdrawn.

"Dealing With" vs. Processing Sensory Input

Early in childhood, there is a critical juncture in human development, where perception of the sensory environment is paramount to our development. Those with ASD are at a crossroads. They must either allow the input to penetrate and then manage the discomfort, or they must block out the input. From a more clinical perspective, it is as though their neurological development takes a bit of a detour from the developmental path of a neuro-typical child, as development works toward managing and reducing input rather than taking in and absorbing it. In other words, "dealing with" input rather than processing it.

When individuals are forced to deal with sensory information that is not being processed accurately, the behavioral manifestations of ASD begin to surface in reaction to their adapting to their sensory surroundings. Their brains are taking in information, but it is either too much or too little and it does not make sense to them. At this point the sensory world becomes overwhelming or even painful. They may find a way to tune out by stimming or by simply shutting off that sensory channel, like the boy whose parents banged pots behind his head did.

Now the outside world begins to see evidence of different types of sensitivities. A parent may notice auditory sensitivities, which are obvious when children plug their ears. I know of many young children who experience auditory hypersensitivities. One young girl, in particular, had significant auditory hypersensitivities. If a bug or insect was flying around her room she could not sleep because it scared her. The only way she could sleep was with headphones on, a box fan running, and a flyswatter in hand (to kill whatever was buzzing around). Not all sounds will necessarily disturb someone with auditory sensitivity. Usually, certain frequencies tend to be bothersome. In the case of this little girl, the buzzing bothered her.

Gastrointestinal or food texture sensitivities may manifest when a child will only eat ice cream, hot dogs, or chicken nuggets from McDonalds. The kids who prefer to be naked are experiencing tactile hypersensitivity. They cannot stand to have clothing touch their skin.

As a child with ASD grows, the child's brain continues to develop, but it develops in a manner so as to block out the overstimulation; he develops a way to cope with, manage, and regulate the overwhelming environment.

Again, what is happening is that the brain cells, or neurons, channel all their energy into coping with or blocking the sensory environment, rather than absorbing and processing the information taken in from that sensory environment. The same amount of effort and energy neuro-typical children devote to taking in and learning about the environment, individuals with ASD devote to dealing with and tuning out the overstimulating features of the environment. So, the brain of someone with ASD is not naturally, automatically creating additional neural pathways and increasing interconnectivity; rather it is developing in a way to limit or manage (i.e., deal with) sensory input.

DEVELOPMENT OF AUTISTIC BEHAVIOR

The continuing development of the brain that is working to cope with and manage sensory hypersensitivity creates a very different neurological architecture than the neuro-typical brain. This anomaly varies the brain's hardwiring drastically. In direct contrast to the neuro-typical brain, which is automatized to take in and process the environment, the autistic brain becomes automatized to tune out the sensory stimulation in order to create a very controlled, consistent environment. This is in part responsible for the development of the odd behaviors associated with autism.

We label these behaviors odd for one reason—they are not like the behaviors we typically see in children without ASD. Behaviors like stimming, rocking, zoning out, rigidity, insistence on sameness, or hyperfocus can be a sign that a child is trying to manage the stimuli in an attempt to control and make sense of the world around him. In practicing these behaviors, children with autism create an environment that is manageable because it is consistent and it is black and white. Therefore, this behavior calms them because they are able to process at a level that makes sense. While creating their own black and white environment, they are also screening out the social environment as that, too, is overwhelming due to its lack of consistency.

Because the brain of a child with ASD devotes much of its developmental energy to learning how to deal with the sensory environment, the energy that would otherwise be used to develop increasing levels of processing stimulus and input, culminating in social learning, is sapped. As a result of their neurology, not only do individuals with ASD develop odd, eccentric behaviors, they begin to develop the one key trait in those with ASD—*pronounced social difficulty.*

Social development is a very complex and challenging process for everyone, but it is especially difficult for those individuals with ASD. Children on the spectrum do not learn from watching those around them; their brains are too busy elsewhere. That is a sharp contrast to the automatic abilities of non-ASD children, who intently watch the social interactions amongst their peers and thereby learn expected behavior automatically. Remember Cece and the four square game?

As a result of not learning (or not caring if they are learning) social norms and behaviors from those around them, children on the spectrum do things like pick their noses in public, dress inappropriately, or engage in other socially unacceptable behavior. They have not deduced from watching other people around them or from the feedback they get when performing these behaviors that what they are doing is unacceptable. They have not developed any social filters.

LANGUAGE DEVELOPMENT/SPEECH

Speech issues are a diagnostic component of spectrum disorders. A young child who falls on the autistic spectrum might not be able to make speechless sounds (e.g., babbling or cooing), or she might have no speech development at all. Language may develop and then become lost at 18 to 24 months. If there is speech development, it may be delayed.

For those on the higher end of the ASD spectrum, language may indeed develop, but it lacks social understanding or pragmatics (an understanding of the relationship between words and expressions). Often, these children learn language from television, movies, computers, and video games. What is so interesting is that they are smart enough to use that language in social contexts. However, if they use a phrase they hear often on TV, they can sound a little odd, rather than naturally spontaneous and responsive to what is going around them. For example, a child might repeat the phrase "What's up, Doc?" every time he enters a room. If he were coming into my office, that expression might not seem to be out of place, but in other environments, such as a classroom, it would be inappropriate. These kids miss the social nuances of language. When I am evaluating someone for ASD, I ask the parents if their child repeats phrases that don't always seem to apply to the situation. If they say yes, I see this as an indicator that the child may be on the spectrum.

SPEECH ISSUES

There are a number of speech pathologies that may be evident in children with ASD. Some kids display *echolalia*, which is mimicking words without any understanding (e.g., repeating commercials or jingles). Children may repeat, verbatim, dialogues from cartoons or movies; they repeat these words or phrases in place of normal responsive language. *Parroting* is another common speech behavior, and is characterized by repeating back what was said. If asked, "What is your name?" the child's response would be, "What is your name?" Pronoun confusion is also common.

Many people on the spectrum experience frustration with their own lack of speech, and/or the inability to communicate their wants and feelings. They may also display difficulty in expressing their needs, using gestures or pointing instead of using words. Laughing (and/or crying) for no apparent reason and showing distress for reasons not apparent to others may also be indicators of difficulty with speech.

ZONING OUT

Zoning out in active environments is also a common reaction. Those on the spectrum will often withdraw into their own world and appear to lose touch with what is going on around them. This can be the result of overstimulation or boredom. It could occur when the child hears a phrase that reminds him of his favorite cartoon. For example, someone could mention the color red, and the ASD child might have seen a cartoon that morning in which his favorite character was wearing a red hat. Hearing the word red could take his mind back to the cartoon, and he could become lost in his own world.

I remember working with a young lady who had attended an assembly at which a man was speaking about the horrible hardships he had suffered in his life and how he had persevered. It was totally quiet while he was speaking when all of a sudden she broke out in laughter. She was not listening and responding to what he was saying, she was in her own world where she was enjoying herself. Individuals on the spectrum may also laugh when they are nervous or are feeling intense emotions. Obviously, this can happen at the most inopportune times.

Zoning out can make the individual look like he is having a seizure. In rare cases, it may be a seizure, but more than likely the individual is focused on something of interest, and is in her own world. Remember, individuals on the spectrum are good at hyperfocusing!

DEVELOPMENT OF SOCIAL UNDERSTANDING

Social interactions are the most neurologically complex tasks we engage in as human beings. For example, many books have been written about how men and women communicate differently, including Dr. John Gray's blockbuster, *Men are from Mars, Women are from Venus*. We know this intuitively and even make fun of the resulting behavior in our society, often pointing out the humor in situations that arise because what a man says means something different to him than to the woman he is speaking to and vice versa. If it's so difficult for neuro-typical individuals to navigate such intricate social interactions, imagine what it is like for someone on the spectrum who takes everything at face value.

Eye contact is another social nuance that causes issues with individuals with ASD; they often struggle with making what individuals without ASD deem appropriate eye contact. I work with many kids who have difficulty with this. Even in infancy, when mom is trying to engage, it can be overwhelming for the baby. Unlike those on the spectrum, those of us who are neuro-typical have automatically learned the cultural norms for eye contact. Staring is one aspect of this.

Imagine sitting in a restaurant and you notice someone staring at you. What do you do? Do you stare back, or do you feel extremely uncomfortable, start to feel flushed, and tell someone next to you, "He is staring at me"? Do you walk over and say, "Hi, I noticed you were looking at me. I thought I would introduce myself"? Probably not. We all have the same tendency, but for those of us without autism, it is just not as pronounced as for those individuals on the spectrum. We know when to look away and when to reengage in eye contact. I find it so interesting to be stuck in a traffic jam and feel the sensation that someone is looking at me. I don't want to look, but I just have that feeling and I have to look. If I do discover that someone is staring at me, I feel uncomfortable because I cannot go anywhere to get away from the staring! Have you ever had that experience?

Depending on what sources you read, one of the most prevalent phobias is public speaking. It is believed that many people are more afraid of speaking in public than of dying. Individuals with ASD don't feel any differently than the rest of us, only they feel it times 10. It is not only public speaking that makes them uncomfortable, but also one-on-one interactions, especially with people they do not know. This dynamic also affects individuals without ASD, but to nowhere near the same degree.

Individuals on the spectrum typically do not understand the social nuances of nonverbal cues, such as eye contact, facial expressions, etc. Keep in mind that, while neuro-typical individuals are in a growth pattern where learning occurs by watching others engage in these activities, individuals with ASD are devoting the same amount of energy and effort to tuning out the environmental stimulation, trying to control the environment, and thus trying to create sameness in their world. Therefore, they have not built up a lifetime of experience to draw upon in interpreting subtle gestures or expressions.

Very high-functioning individuals with ASD can and do learn to engage in one-on-one interactions on some level, but as the number of people involved in a situation increases, so does the complexity of the situation, and so does the discomfort of the person with ASD.

DEVELOPMENT OF LINEAR PROCESSING/BLACK AND WHITE THINKING

As you begin to understand the need for an individual with autism to control input, you will see that black and white thinking and linear processing make more sense as a strategy to organize and understand the world. The black and white, linear thinking that is so prevalent for people on the spectrum is driven by the individual's desire to create *sameness* (i.e., the need to make new information fit into an existing framework so that it is easier to process).

Temple Grandin feels that individuals with autism process things either in pictures or numbers. Temple feels that she, herself, processes things in pictures. Regardless of whether an individual processes in pictures or numbers, this is a very linear way to make sense of the world. I created a diagram (6.1) based on her description of how she thinks and processes her environment as well as on my clinical work with individuals on the spectrum.

It is difficult to manage a gray, ever-changing environment with a system that is designed to see only black and white. For example, Temple describes her own experience in processing the word *dog*. She sees a picture in her head of the first visual representation of that word that she can remember, which is her German shepherd from her childhood. Since her first experience with a dog, every time she hears the word *dog*, she sees that same picture of her shepherd in her head. This is very different from what individuals without autism process in their brains when they hear the word *dog*. The following diagram

NEUROLOGICAL DOG DIAGRAM

Normal Individual   Individual with ASD

Processing the Word *Dog*   Processing the Word *Dog*

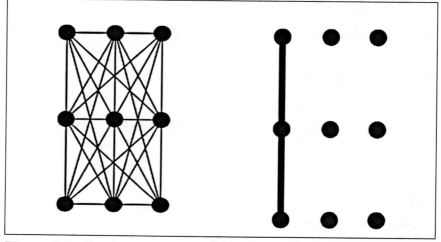

Diagram 6.1 - The dots represent neurons and the lines represent axons and dendrites communicating amongst the neurons. The left side of the diagram represents what the neurons of those not on the spectrum would be doing when they hear the word **dog,** and the right side represents what fires neurologically in the brain of an individual with autism when she hears the word **dog.**

illustrates the contrast in brain interconnectivity and the resulting inflexibility in individuals with and without autism.

Neuro-typical individuals can think in a linear fashion in this case as well. They might think of the first time they heard the word *dog* and how they correlated the word with the animal. They might think of the dog that almost bit them, or they might think about an advertisement of a dog they recently saw. The difference is that when they hear an abstract word, like *dog,* the neurons in their brains fire making numerous connections until those individuals reach a decision to think in a linear mode by quantifying the information requested. So, as the result of their highly developed neurological interconnectivity, non-ASD individuals can adapt immediately from nonlinear to linear thinking and back again. The challenge for those on the spectrum is that they cannot operate both ways like their neuro-typical friends. Temple's brain does not see the gray area—she needs to take the information and put it into a black and white filter in order to interpret it. From this vantage point, it is easy to understand the compartmentalized black and white thinking of a person on the spectrum.

Temple explains that when she engages in conversation with someone, she plays "videotapes" in her brain, searching for the correct existing response to use. This is happening in the midst of a conversation! Her brain attempts to make a conversation black and white. I remember watching her give a presentation years ago. She was using a slide carousel, but someone else was advancing the slides for her. Every time she wanted the slide changed, she would say, "Next slide please." She never used any other phrase to request that the slides be changed—through an entire presentation. I remember that it did begin to get monotonous every time she said, "Next slide please." She was doing a nice job with the presentation but it was very information driven and not very entertaining; she did not add any humor or tell any jokes. This type of behavior may appear very odd in the neuro-typical world.

This particular presentation included a luncheon. Temple was scheduled to answer questions at about 11:45 a.m.; we were scheduled to eat lunch at noon. I could not believe how well she responded to the questions; she even made eye contact. Then a staff member approached her and whispered into her ear. Temple immediately said, "Thank you very much" and sat down at her table to eat lunch. It was one of those awkward moments—the audience was expecting her to continue answering questions. She just sat down, placed her napkin on her lap, and started drinking her water. What happened, I would guess, was that the information communicated to her was not black and white, it was gray information (the staff member who approached her must have said that she needed to wrap up soon, shortly, or in a few minutes); Temple needed to make it black and white, which resulted in her taking control of the situation and abruptly ending the presentation.

I have seen Temple present more recently, and now she does tell jokes and she uses a PowerPoint presentation. She doesn't laugh at any of her jokes, she just pauses while the audience laughs, and then she continues. She has learned to adapt to the neuro-typical world's expectations of a presentation.

At a different conference at which we were both presenting, someone asked her why she did not open a school for autism, or work with kids and families that are touched by autism. She answered very matter-of-factly, "Because I work with cattle." While we were sitting together at lunch, Temple suddenly stood up and said, "I have to sign books. It is 12:30." The door closed behind her before I could say goodbye to her. Temple is clearly predisposed to be a black and white thinker.

The lack of interconnectivity neurologically underlies this tendency to be inflexible in one's thinking; when concepts are deeply ingrained, as they are in children with ASD, it is very difficult to change the minds of these children. This is the root of their rigidity. That makes initial exposure to a concept an especially critical moment of opportunity for a parent or educator. Once the concepts are established in the child's mind, they will likely be very difficult to change.

DEVELOPMENT OF EXECUTIVE FUNCTIONING

Most kids on the spectrum struggle with executive functioning, which is the ability to learn from past experiences and apply world knowledge. This ability allows us to evaluate an action in advance and draw a conclusion, anticipate outcomes, and adapt to changing situations. This is the brain function that manages goal-directed activity.

Poor development of executive functioning is related to the black and white thinking and lack of interconnectivity for individuals with ASD. Their linear thinking impairs their ability to see any connection between their behavior and the consequences they are likely to experience. For example, if someone with ASD decides to pick up a rock and throw it through a window, he may not be able to correlate the outcome of having to pay for a replacement window with the act of throwing the rock. He throws the rock and is surprised by the consequences. I discuss executive functioning in more detail in Chapter 7, Understanding Autistic Processing.

Many kids are forgetful, but kids with ASD can be forgetful times 10. Some are challenged with attention deficit disorder (ADD) or attention-deficit/hyperactivity disorder (ADHD) tendencies, which result in memory issues. In addition, a child on the spectrum is probably not motivated by some of the factors that help other children to make choices about their behavior. For example, typically children on the spectrum are not motivated to please their teachers or fit in with the other kids in the class. They simply lack the intrinsic motivation. Compounded with their lack of awareness or inability to remember long-term goals, executive functioning becomes an issue for many of these children.

When executive functioning is a challenge, a child often arrives to class, but without the proper supplies (books, pencils, etc.) or without his homework, and he is unaware of the long-term consequences of that behavior. He cannot make the leap from building good study and work habits in seventh grade to getting the job he may want someday. For him to make that connection, someone would have to explain the consequences of his choices. Learning good study habits today increases the likelihood of good grades in high school, which, in turn, makes getting into the college program of his choice easier, which may ultimately lead to the job of his dreams in the future.

Another example is a little boy who loved playing games at school recess. He was so into it, that he got very angry when he lost, and he would punch other kids. He continued to conduct himself in this manner time and time again. As a result, he was not allowed to participate in recess. He was unable to piece together the cause and effect between his actions and the consequence of missing out on recess. This concept of accountability as it ties to executive functioning will be expanded on in Chapter 8, Understanding Characterisitics of ASD.

DEVELOPMENT OF ANXIETY, DEPRESSION, AND OBSESSIVE/COMPULSIVE TENDENCIES

Keep in mind that as individuals with ASD are developing neurologically, they are motivated to tune out the external environment in order to eliminate overstimulation and maintain a sense of calm. In their attempt to control the environment, individuals with autism learn to create "sameness." If I inhabited a world in which change was very painful, but that world was always changing, I would want to try to control it, too, by attempting to make it the same every single day. This is what starts to happen in the brain of a child with autism. To cope, they frequently become experts in sameness.

These attempts to control the environment become increasingly difficult for children on the spectrum. As they grow up, their lives become more complex and the world expects more from them. Ultimately, their need for sameness and society's demands for flexibility and adaptability conflict. This leads to a great deal of anxiety, depression, and, often, obsessive-compulsive tendencies. Anger is also prevalent, but I will address that further in Chapter 11, Coping with Anger.

We can logically understand how the desperate need for control and sameness in an ever-changing world would give rise to anxiety. The result of the pervasive disappointment that they experience daily can also lead to depression.

While I recognize the fact that there are physiological and biological causes for depression, I believe that most of the kids I treat who experience depression are coping with *situational depression*, which, as its name implies, is caused by life's situations (for example, living in a world not designed for you). Unlike those of us who have accepted that we have to go to work every day even though we would prefer to do otherwise, individuals on the spectrum do not have the flexibility to adjust their thinking. This inability to always accept doing what they do not want to do leads to situational depression, which can be as debilitating and painful as clinical or major depression.

Obsessive-compulsive disorder (OCD) also stems from a great deal of anxiety. Individuals who develop OCD, whether they have autism or not, are making an attempt to control the environment around them because of their anxiety. They control either their thoughts (obsessions) or their actions (compulsions). Obsessive-compulsive individuals will try to control the environment, thinking that they can calm themselves if they do something, but they have to do it perfectly. For example, if an individual believes he has germs on him, he will wash and wash and wash until he feels comfortable. This lowers his anxiety.

Although individuals with autism seem to develop OCD tendencies for similar reasons as those without autism, they are different psychologically. An individual with a diagnosis of OCD does not necessarily have autism, although individuals with autism can have OCD tendencies.

Individuals without autism who have a diagnosis of OCD will admit that their obsession or compulsion is silly. Those on the spectrum do not feel that their OCD behaviors are silly at all; they feel compelled to act this way, often getting very upset if someone tries to stop them from engaging in what they feel is a necessary behavior. Anxiety and obsessive tendencies in individuals with ASD can be very pronounced. Refer to Appendix C for information on how to manage OCD with medication.

HOW THE AUTISTIC NEUROLOGICAL ARCHITECTURE IMPACTS BEHAVIOR

It is difficult to separate an individual's behavior from his autistic neurological architecture as it has been described in the previous chapters. It is the actual neurological structure, the way the minds of spectrum individuals are built, which gives rise to their behavior. As the result of this neurology, the brains of individuals with autism spectrum disorders develop into inflexible, black and white, static linear systems. This linear system could be characterized as a means-to-an-end system; one that is focused on getting basic needs met (physical comfort such as food, warmth, and shelter, as opposed to emotional comfort). It is incredibly stressful for people with ASD when these basic needs are not met. This makes their drive and determination very intense, and their resulting behavior very driven to that end—which is not wrong, just different.

Individuals without ASD have a more flexible, abstract, dynamic evolving system; it is ever changing and adapting. The best way to describe the non-ASD neurological architecture is that it is a social system, which is characterized by the flexibility to both interpret the need for change and to respond to constant change.

For example, in a social setting, such as a gathering of kids after school, the topic of conversation usually changes, the location may change, and the people involved in the conversation may vary. The more people involved, the more complex the situation becomes, and the more fluid the conversation. Individuals without ASD are able to go with the flow of the conversation, riding life's waves comfortably and naturally. People on the spectrum find maneuvering this terrain very confusing and challenging, if not painful, due to their neurological architecture, which makes them unable to effectively follow and interpret social information.

The difference between operating with the socially based neurological architecture of someone who is neuro-typical and operating with the linear, nonsocial architecture common to those with ASD is huge. It impacts almost every aspect of daily life. It is very difficult to tease the social elements out of many situations, because they exist almost everywhere.

Unlike those with ASD, non-ASD individuals constantly think about how their behavior impacts others and how to adjust that behavior. Those with ASD don't have that same social approach. They are neither assessing their behavior to the same degree socially, nor are they attempting to modify their behavior to fit in with others.

HOW NEUROLOGICAL ARCHITECTURE IMPACTS INFORMATION PROCESSING

If we accept the notion that individuals with autism are overloaded by the sensory environment, that it is not only overstimulating, it is also, in many cases, uncomfortable, and that they devote most (if not all) of their energy to dealing with this dilemma, then that begs the question, "What impact does that have on the way they think and process information?"

As previously stated, a child's brain does not stop developing just because he faces overload from the environmental stimulus. Since developing dynamically would overstress his neurology (i.e., he can't develop dynamically due to his lack of neurological interconnectivity), he improvises, finding different concrete ways to manage the stimulus such as organizing, categorizing, memorizing, and reducing things to black and white terms.

The need for the world to be black and white manifests in behaviors that are used as diagnostic criteria for ASD. Think about the child who lines up objects. Why is she doing this? What could she possibly like about lining up 37 cars in her room? This is a concrete activity, so it makes sense to her. This behavior serves two purposes for children on the spectrum. First, it is calming because of the consistent nature of the activity; it is an activity that they can control. Second, they are able to use it to tune out any external stimulation. They hyperfocus on the activity, tune out what is going on around them, create a more orderly world, and thus calm themselves.

I remember noticing that my first client with autism, 2-year-old Stevie, would line up his toy cars on the floor. I realized that this activity seemed to calm him (I did not understand autism in the same way then that I do today). If someone moved one of the cars, Stevie would yell, "No, no, no!" and immediately place the car back in its place. In order to feel comfortable, Stevie needed the cars to be lined up exactly as he had placed them.

Things that are consistent and never change reduce anxiety in everyone, but especially in individuals with ASD. Information that is consistent is reliable and makes sense in a world that is constantly changing and, therefore, feels unreliable. Individuals on the spectrum crave the black and white, concrete, nongray input and surroundings (sameness) in order to feel in control of the environment. That is a very linear way of processing, one that is radically different from the nonlinear social approach of neuro-typical individuals.

Remember, sensory volume in individuals with ASD is magnified times 10 and the resulting reaction to drown out the noise must also be magnified times 10 to be proportionate. In order to manage the stimulus, they work very hard to create a very consistent, black and white environment. Hence, their rigid and extreme need to line up objects, for example. While the downside of their intense focus may appear as a rigid things-a-certain-way behavior, the same quality and intensity leads them to be 10 times better at what they focus on than their non-ASD friends. This explains some of the incredible talent they display.

Keep in mind that, unlike their neuro-typical peers, individuals with ASD are not exploring the environment and establishing inter-connectivity among their neurons. Their brains become automatized (habitually acclimated) to making sense of information in the environment that is consistent, linear and structured. They process and understand information that is concrete, such as the placement of objects in a room, the route from one place to another, or the months on a calendar. While noticing these consistencies, they are calming themselves and creating a sense of order. As more and more neurons are differentiated to process structured information, their brains are becoming more rigid, while the brains of their neuro-typical peers are developing the capacity to absorb more and more information, thus becoming more flexible.

STATIC PROCESSING AND EXPERIENCE

An individual with autism has a processing system that can be de-scribed as nonflexible, static linear approach. This is not meant as a value judgment; this type of processing is not wrong—it's just differ-ent. We can all process in a linear way; everybody reading this book is doing it. As a matter of fact, sometimes processing in a linear fashion is relaxing. When we are stressed, coming back to something that is consistent is calming, like coming home after a long day's work. So processing using a static system is a means to an end; it is very linear and organized, and therefore comforting to a child.

Dynamic processing—processing that is ever changing, non-[...] and designed to embrace the unknown—is not as hard for those of us without ASD because we are not using as much neurological energy to process our environment in comparison to those on the spectrum. We have automatized this capability. Therefore, we're not driven to linear thinking in an effort to conserve neurological energy that is needed to simply manage our sense of overload from what is going on around us. We have the neurological interconnectivity to fluidly follow the input from the world around us. Our dynamic system absorbs, processes, and updates continually; we are constantly and automatically responding to a world that is always changing.

The difference between the two approaches has an enormous impact on experience. Think about going to a party. Those of us without ASD might think, "I wonder who is going to be there. I'm excited because I don't know. Maybe I'll see some friends." That's an interesting and positive feeling—there's anticipation about the possibilities. However, a child on the spectrum might be thinking, "I don't want to go unless I know everybody who will be there. What are we going to do? What are we going to do first?" Her desire is to have no surprises so that the stimulus is linear and, therefore, not overwhelming.

The rule of thumb that I follow is this: the positive, exciting anxiety that we experience for the unknown (like the excitement about going to a party) is completely the opposite experience for those on the spectrum. For example, the Christmas presents that are exciting for my kids can be a source of discomfort for kids on the spectrum. My kids are thinking, "I can't wait to open those! I wonder what's in them. Can you give me a hint?" Some children on the spectrum will say, "Why are those wrapped? You're really trying to cause me some discomfort here, aren't you? You've got something in there, and you're not telling me what it is; now, I won't be able to sleep tonight."

One child told me that it bothered him so much that he did not know what was in a Christmas gift one year; he tried very hard to figure out what it was. In order to calm himself down, he decided that he knew what it was. When he opened the present on Christmas morning what he expected, he became so distressed as day, even though he liked the present. This w a linear, static approach affects a child's beha-sy to see how this need for order could give rise to ot well received socially. Imagine how frustrating and as to his parents to see his negative reaction to their gift.

esult of their static processing, children on the spectrum exp. ce life from a completely different perspective—a perspective that we should keep in mind when we're thinking about therapy, having interactions, and talking with these kids. That perspective needs to shape our expectations of them.

THE IMPACT OF STATIC PROCESSING ON SOCIAL UNDERSTANDING

The stimulus-processing difficulties of children on the spectrum negatively impact their social understanding. In order to process social interactions efficiently and completely, an individual must be functioning in the environment automatically (i.e., automatized, not cognitively focused on processing). The greater the difficulty in processing the environment, the more energy is expended on managing lower level input, resulting in fewer resources being available to effectively process the higher level input of the social interaction.

In a one-on-one conversation, there is only one other person, or variable, involved. Adding a second person doubles the variables, as does changing the topic, or introducing new information. Each variable increases the complexity of a social interaction exponentially. That complexity, combined with the difficulty the ASD individual has processing the sensory input, makes it very likely that the subtleties and implications of each individual social interaction will be lost. Therefore, as social complexity increases, it will become very difficult, if not impossible, for the mind of someone on the spectrum to process and fully understand the social interaction. Hence, the frequently heard expression, "unable to pick up on social cues."

THE IMPACT OF STATIC PROCESSING ON FUNCTIONALITY

People processing in a static system can still live a full life; they can still be functional. They may need to adapt by using visuals, numbers, or schedules to piece things together in a way that makes sense to them. That is how they will take an environment that is inherently dynamic and create a linear environment that is functional for them.

One of the trickiest aspects of making these adjustments is that children on the spectrum need to do this without appearing too odd. As I have already mentioned, they need to fit into our society to a certain degree in order to be functional and survive. As they become adults, it is important to make sure they can work at a place of employment where they can follow the rules and can shift gears from one task to another when they need to. When their boss says, "Stop doing what you are doing and do this," they must be able to stop and do something different even if they do not want to.

When I was working at a warehouse (one of the many jobs I held while paying my way through school) I met a co-worker named Pete. Pete's job was to unload shipments from the trucks, sort return bottles in the warehouse, and reload the empty bottles onto the trucks. Most of the time, he just sorted the empties—the 16-ounce pint bottles; he would unload and load trucks once or twice a week. Pete was very methodical. When I first started work at this warehouse, my boss said to me, "Look at this, Tim," showing me Pete's timecard. Every day at 8:00 a.m., within a minute, he punched in, and every day at 4:30 p.m., within a minute, he punched out.

I drove a delivery route for awhile and I'd come back to the warehouse and I'd ask, "Pete can you help me?" He'd reply, "Nope, not my job." And he'd pass by me really slowly on the forklift. "Come on Pete, just bring me a couple of things I need. I've got to get back out!" "Not my job," he'd say, and he'd go by really slowly. When a truck that he was supposed to unload would pull in at 4:20 p.m., he'd break out in a sweat. Pete would become very upset because he would not be able to go home at 4:30 and this threw his schedule off; it would break his routine if he had to stay later.

that he hired Pete because he saw him working at
ght; he witnessed the staff making fun of him and
ı time (social difficulty?). He told Pete that he could
.ehouse if he wanted to, and that no one would make
ete was in his mid-30s when he started working for my
ᴄ .e still lived at home with his mom; he was relatively
functᴄ.. at work.

Individuals with ASD can be productive in the right environment, at the right job, and with the right job coaching. Fortunately, the neuro-typical world is becoming more familiar with (and accommodating to) the world of those on the spectrum. I have a lot of hope for the kids I see. Through therapy, we try to help them learn to function effectively and fit in enough to find a way to carve out a happy, satisfying life for themselves. I like to focus on the strengths associated with autism and teach them to use these strengths to help them handle their challenges. I feel they need to embody their autism, learn about it, and figure out how to function in life. Remember, autism itself is not wrong; it is just a different way of looking at and processing the world.

CHAPTER 7

UNDERSTANDING
AUTISTIC PROCESSING ADAPTATIONS

The rigid thinking of the autistic mind makes it very difficult for individuals on the spectrum to do things they don't want to do, and life is full of times when we need this skill to be functional.

When the environment around individuals with ASD presents a great enough processing challenge, or threatens to cause overload, they attempt to control it to make it easier for them to comprehend. In order to do this, their brains are forced to create an environment that makes sense to them. As a result, the following processing adaptations ensue:

1. Black and white thinking
2. Rigid thinking
3. Getting stuck
4. Becoming experts in sameness
5. Literal thinking (difficulties with metaphors)

These concepts were presented earlier, but they are so vital to understanding the thinking of a child on the spectrum that they warrant further discussion. Not all children display all of these processing anomalies, nor do any two individuals have them to the same degree or manifest them in the same way. By understanding these in a simple form, as a parent or teacher, you can monitor how they play out in your child's behavior. Keep in mind that every child is unique and that personality comes first.

BLACK AND WHITE THINKING

A common trait that requires more understanding is the tendency toward black and white processing. This way of thinking is consistent with all-or-none thinking—all good or all bad—or any form of categorizing things in extremes. If you were to evaluate how your day went on a continuum between good or bad, those of us who are optimistic might say, for the most part, our days are good. Diagram 7.1 shows a good and bad continuum.

We all experience days of one extreme or the other: our best days ever, which, for me, would be when my children were born; and our worst days, which, for me, were the days I have lost loved ones. I am an optimistic person; to me, every day is a good day, some are just better than others.

Diagram 7.1 is drawn from the perspective of an autistic individual, who sees only black and white. There is a characteristic absence of the gray area between the two. For those on the spectrum who exhibit all-or-none thinking, everything falls into either a "good" box or a "bad" box (while the rest of us live in between, in the abstract gray area). As long as the activity happening around them is perceived by them as good, it falls in the box at the good end of the diagram. The size of the good box can change depending on the individual, with some seeing more events as being good. The size of the good box can also vary from day to day for one individual based on how well things are going that day. They also can have days that nothing seems to fit into the good box, where the good box is very small, i.e., bad days.

The problem arises when these children on the spectrum perceive something as not falling in their good box. Given black and white thinking, there is only one other option—the bad box. For example, a child perceives that correctly answering all the questions on a test is good. When he gets his test back and there is one answer wrong, he has a meltdown because this is not what he perceives as good. Therefore, he responds as if it is really bad. The emotional response is disproportionate to the magnitude of the incident (i.e., missing one question on a test) because the event took him all the way to the opposite end of the continuum where the bad box is located. It's very hard, if not impossible, for someone practicing black and white thinking to see the middle ground. Everything is managed by being placed at either one extreme or the other. Falling in between or being in both simultaneously is not even perceived as possible by a black and white thinker.

One day, a young man came to my office after school claiming to have had the worst day ever. I asked him what happened, and he said that someone had bumped into him in the hall. He even admitted that the other boy bumped him accidentally. I asked, "Okay, this is the worst day ever. What else happened that was bad today?" He looked at me and said, "Nothing else bad happened today." He had simply been

HOW TO VISUALIZE BLACK AND WHITE THINKING

Good   Bad

Diagram 7.1 - Individuals on the autistic spectrum view the world in black and white. Everything is either all good or all bad. There is no in-between, no gray area.

bumped by accident in the hall, and that ruined his day, taking him (in his mind) from the good box to the bad box with no stops in between.

Through therapy, I showed him how his perceptions of his overall day did not equate to how the day actually went. I created two lists: a good/neutral category and a bad category. I had to create a good/neutral category to have a category other than bad. I added neutral primarily because he would not see very much about school as being good. I asked him to recall incidents that happened during the day, and in which category of the two he felt each event would fall in. After we made the lists, we had 14 events in the good/neutral category, and only one event in the bad category. I put the lists in front of him, and then asked him again, based on this data, how he perceived his day now. He responded, "I guess it was not that bad." I find that when data is presented in such a concrete way to a child on the spectrum, it is an insult to their black and white linear thinking, and this helps them to find the gray area.

RIGID THINKING

Many of the flexibilities that life requires are very difficult for people with autism spectrum disorder due to their rigid thinking. Rigid thinking starts with the overstimulation of the sensory processing system. The brain is forced to deal with this, and the only way to do so is to attempt to control it. This control creates further limitation of interconnectivity, which increases the need to control. This process snowballs, and in doing so, it stifles further expansion of the interconnectivity. This is not happening at a conscious level. It is not a conscious choice, but rather the brain's adaptation to the processing and sensory difficulties.

It is the rigid thinking of the autistic mind that makes it so hard for individuals on the spectrum to do something that they don't want to do, and life is full of times when we need this skill to be functional. Most neuro-typical kids don't want to brush their teeth, but they are able to learn to do it consistently because they have the flexibility to do so. Those on the spectrum may never be able to learn this without the help of extrinsic motivation (or the parents enforcing the rules).

Neuro-typical individuals can also be very rigid thinkers, although it is not as common for them as it is for those on the spectrum, nor is it diagnostic. For example, one of my closest friends is incredibly staunch in his political views, and whole-heartedly backs his chosen political party's beliefs. In a matter of a few sentences, I can get him totally worked up when it comes to politics. I know just what to say to get him going. Let's just say he is very, very committed to his perspective in politics. There is no way, no matter what I say, that I could change his thinking so that he could pledge allegiance to the opposing political party. He has spent his entire adult life thinking and believing this way. I would have to rebuild his personality from the ground up to shift his loyalty to the other side. His perceptions represent this type of inflexibility.

Although my friend does not face the same neurological barriers, his entrenched thinking and his level of commitment to his political views are similar to the kind of rigid thinking I see in kids on the spectrum. The difference with my friend is that, in other areas of his life, he can evaluate and be flexible as well as social. That is to say, he is not rigid or stuck in other areas. With those on the spectrum, this rigidity could potentially happen with any subject matter! I remember when this same friend got into a hot political debate with another friend of ours. He ended up laughing and apologizing about the whole thing. Someone with ASD could never step back and escape his rigid thinking, or see it as over the top.

Here's another example that gives you the flavor of how difficult changes in thinking can be for our friends on the spectrum. I am from North Dakota, therefore I am a Vikings fan. My friends in Illinois are mostly Bears fans. No matter what I say or do, no matter how good the Vikings play, I could never convert my friends to become Vikings fans. They are rigid Bears fans. Change in our beliefs is difficult under the best neurological circumstances; change is difficult *times 10* for those on the spectrum, whose neurology predisposes them to think in a rigid

yet, for those on the spectrum, the challenge is magnified
their rigidity is not isolated to a manageable number of
, but rather, it is compounded by the fact that they can
inflexible about anything or everything! Their potential
on anything often leads to getting stuck.

"GETTING STUCK"

Behaviorally, "getting stuck" resembles a stubborn, rigid, unrelenting
attitude that often gives rise to angry outbursts, tantrums, rude demands, bipolar tendencies, or other socially unacceptable behavior.
Getting stuck as an autistic adaptation is, often, simply hyperfocus.
The underlying reason these individuals might get stuck could be one
of any number of issues.

For example, they could be so deeply engrained in a black and white
thinking pattern that any other perspective is impossible for them to
see. Their rigid thinking may be at work, or they may be using that
particular thought to calm themselves. It is important to understand
that a major reason for getting stuck is the tremendous anxiety that is
caused when their position is challenged. Another major factor is the
need to control (discussed further in Chapter 9, Anxiety and Control).

Recently, I met with a man who ran a successful farm. He and his
son were having a disagreement about how to water the plants around
the house. One hose was not long enough to reach all the way around
the house; the father wanted the son to work his way around one side
of the house and then go back to where he started and work his way
around the other side of the house, using only one length of hose. The
son had decided to simply use two lengths of hose to get all the way
around the house in one trip.

The dad spent 20 minutes in my office explaining why that was not
a good strategy (it would damage the plants, weigh too much, etc.).
While he was explaining his position to his son, I wrote down on a
piece of paper my prediction of what the son would say. When the dad
had finished explaining to his son why he should use one hose instead

of two, he was red-faced and worn out. I asked the dad what he thought his son would do the next time he watered the plants around the house. He replied, "He will surely use one hose." I then asked the son what was he going to do the next time, and he simply stated, "Use the two lengths of hose together." His father was floored; he could not understand why his son would not comply with his way of thinking, given all the evidence.

To this young man, there was no other option in his mind—he could not see any other way to accomplish the task, and trying any other approach caused him too much anxiety. I asked the dad to read my note and my prediction was dead on; the son was stuck on his first vision of how to do it. When he asked me how I knew what his son would say, I replied that he was stuck. His rigid thinking rendered him unable to view this new perspective, make sense of the data, and adapt to using only one hose.

An individual with autism described to me that once his brain begins to move in a certain direction, it is very hard to stop it from continuing in that direction. People on the spectrum have difficulty creating new neurological pathways. As a result, the importance of a child's first exposure to a concept, activity, or experience becomes critical to their long-term use of (or belief about) that concept. Remember the discussion of the word *dog*? Once the first neurological pathway is created, it is very, very difficult to over-write that mental programming. It can be done, but it can take a long time for someone on the spectrum.

Another gentleman with whom I worked corroborated the difficulty with mental reprogramming. When he was a child first learning the alphabet, he had learned two letters incorrectly, switching their order. At 42 years old, he still had problems reciting the alphabet. This same man told me that it was very hard for him to be flexible enough to change his thinking. When someone gave him incorrect directions, it was extremely difficult for him to correct them in his mind and go the right way after he had initially learned the directions the wrong way. His mind wanted to default to the original directions.

Being stuck might also occur if the individual is using the particular thought that he happens to be stuck on to calm himself or to manage the incoming input. To attempt to change that way of thinking might feel very threatening, as if it would rock the entire delicate emotional balance he has achieved.

To think in terms of gray (i.e., not black or white) can also create tremendous anxiety. I have seen many kids totally stuck on the idea that they are right. Due to their black and white thinking, being wrong about something would threaten their entire view of the world and could collapse their self-esteem, making them believe that since they are no longer good, they are all bad.

Teachers sometimes tell me that they struggle with a student because the child won't do things a certain way in their classrooms. When I ask a teacher why it is important to do it that particular way, and he tells me that it is because he has done it that way for 30 years, I know that this teacher and his student are going to have a very long and frustrating year. Meeting the rigidly stuck mind of a child on the spectrum with equally rigid thinking is not a successful strategy. It is much more effective to understand how and why these individuals get stuck, to try to meet them where they are mentally, and to help them to see other possibilities.

EXPERTS IN SAMENESS

Imagine the discomfort these kids experience living a linear life in a nonlinear world. It's like being dropped into a foreign land that is totally unfamiliar to you. The language is incomprehensible, the customs are all different, the cars travel on the wrong side of the road, and the people are unfamiliar. Communicating with the natives doesn't make any sense, so you are in a constant state of confusion and uncertainty about what is going on around you. This could be incredibly stressful for a fully functioning adult who may have chosen to go to this foreign land on purpose.

Now imagine how frightening that scenario would be if you were a child, without adult experience, skills, or reason to help you manage the situation and get your needs met. Here's the real kicker—imagine that everything was notched up times 10! I'd be totally freaked out if the sun were 10 times more intense, the lights were 10 times brighter, colors were 10 times more vibrant, smells were 10 times more pungent, noises were 10 times louder, and everything went 10 times faster. This is what it might feel like to be a child dealing with autism on a daily basis.

If those were the conditions I was living in, I would look for ways to create sameness and grab tightly to anything familiar, too. It makes sense, then, given their sensitivity to stimuli, that these kids become very committed to organizing the environment to create consistency. Consistency that is familiar is, therefore, comforting. Have you ever been lost? When you are lost and unsure of where you are, doesn't recognizing something familiar provide instant relief?

With their attention focused on finding sameness, these kids become very good at recognizing consistencies in the environment. Sameness can pertain to objects or routines, anything that provides stability. From this vantage point, it is easy to see why this practice would be both calming and enjoyable at the same time.

It's just amazing how intently some of these kids can focus on the detail. I recently evaluated a little boy who was potentially on the spectrum. For our initial meeting, I met with him and both his parents in my office, where, on the windowsill, I display objects built of Legos that young clients have made for me during therapy. This little boy walked in six weeks after our first and only meeting, barely stepped into my office, and said, "Is that a new Lego?" I looked to check (because I didn't remember, even though I see them every day) and I realized that what he was referring to was, indeed, a new Lego figure that had been built since his last visit. It was truly amazing that he could instantly pick up on that.

You see, when he was in my office the first time, he was focused on the physical things, which helped him calm down and tune out the stimulation that was creating anxiety or uneasiness. Many kids on the spectrum, looking for sameness, focus on the details and calm themselves in this way. So, imagine living in a world that feels chaotic, and suddenly discovering that the calendar was never changing. That would be very calming—an island of sanity in a sea of confusion. That is the same reason the placement of objects in the room is important to these kids—it is familiar, therefore, it is calming.

Years ago, I treated a young man with Asperger's disorder who started therapy around the holidays. The reason he came to see me was that his parents had put up a Christmas tree in the living room and he was having a lot of difficulty with the change in the furniture placement in that room. When I asked him about it, he said he was upset because the couch had moved two feet and he liked to read on the couch. I asked him if anything else had changed about the couch that made it harder for him to read. Was the lighting different? Did it face a different direction? Did the couch feel different to sit in? He said, "No, the couch moved two feet." That's it! The only difference was the position of the couch in the room.

Therapeutically, we managed to deal with the change. I decided to ask him if he was going to have a Christmas tree in his house when he was older, since this seemed to be so difficult for him to manage. I loved his response, which was, "Yes, I am going to build a nook that sticks out of the living room that I will put the tree in." I asked him what he was going to put in the nook when it was not Christmas time and guess what he replied? "Nothing. That is where the tree goes."

I truly believe that if he is able to create a nook in his house in the future, he will do it. The only thing that will ever be in the nook will be a Christmas tree. There will be an official day in November when the tree goes up, and an official day after Christmas when tₕₑ comes down. Nothing else will ever go into that nook. This story exemplifies the autistic drive for control and sameness. It also clearly demonstrates how an autistic mind adapts and creates solutions that fit the need for linear input.

The drive for sameness can impact any arena of life. I have worked with kids who would literally eat chicken nuggets from McDonald's for every meal because they craved that sameness. Another child didn't want to have a new teacher in the fall, even though he hated the teacher he had. He would rather keep the familiar teacher he hated than cope with the change. One boy had a dry erase board in his room, and he kept the markers lined up. He was so particular about his room that if even one marker was moved, he became upset. That's what I mean when I describe that linear emphasis on sameness; kids with autism are experts in sameness.

LITERAL THINKING/DIFFICULTY WITH METAPHORS AND SLANG

In spoken language, we use metaphors and slang all the time. In my office, I avoid using figurative language because it is difficult for many on the spectrum to understand. Most people with autism are very, very literal.

I worked with a boy named Phil who has an IQ of about 120 and plays in the orchestra. One day his mom told me, "He was so excited to perform in the school concert. It was like he was walking on clouds when he walked to his seat." Phil heard his mom make that comment, and he responded, "No, I wasn't. Mom, I wasn't walking on clouds. I was on the gym floor." Phil couldn't comprehend that his mother was using a metaphor. He was stuck trying to translate that statement literally. His mother said, "Phil, that was just an expression that meant that you were very happy and excited for the concert."

We have to be careful with metaphors because, in the real world, we will use them and not even realize we're doing it. We lose them with language like "walking on clouds." Then, we continue on in the conversation while they're still stuck. Phil responded to his mother by saying, "Yeah, but you cannot walk on clouds, Mom. Why would you say that?" Imagine how hard it is for him to communicate with his peers when they use slang that he interprets literally.

If you say to a child on the spectrum, "We're going to Grandma's house," and you stop at a gas station on the way, you'll end up with a child having a meltdown. Why? Because the gas station isn't Grandma's house. "Going to Grandma's" is not the same as "going to the gas station and then going to Grandma's." Individuals with ASD are very literal.

As I mentioned at the beginning of this chapter (and repeat here because it is so important), the underlying dynamics that drive some of the most typical behaviors and attitudes of those on the spectrum include these five processing adaptations: 1) black and white thinking; 2) rigid thinking; 3) getting stuck; 4) becoming experts in sameness; and 5) literal thinking. These dynamics can be at play individually or they can be so intertwined that it is difficult to identify the threads of each separately. Identifying and understanding how they play out in your child's life will go a long way toward reducing the child's overall anxiety level. Most important, remember that every child is unique and that personality comes first.

CHAPTER 8

UNDERSTANDING CHARACTERISTICS OF ASD

If you can only remember one thing about interpreting behavior, remember that all behavior serves a purpose of some sort—all behavior is communication.

F iguring out why a certain behavior is occurring can be a very challenging task when working with individuals on the spectrum. Parents and educators who can decipher what a particular behavior is communicating can unlock the key to understanding a child with ASD and how best to work with that child.

BEHAVIOR AS COMMUNICATION

If you can only remember one thing about interpreting behavior, remember that all behavior serves a purpose of some sort—all behavior is communication. Understanding the *why* behind the behavior is the key to helping the child.

Finding the reason behind a child's behavior also makes it much easier on the child. A simple way to remember this strategy is to always look at the ABC of a situation—the antecedent, the behavior, and the consequences. The antecedents are the events and circumstances that surround or precede the behavior. By consequences, I am referring to the consequences in the child's mind—not resulting real-world repercussions. What purpose does the behavior serve for the child?

For example, from the child's perspective, he thinks, "I'm overwhelmed, so I need to run out of the classroom." The antecedent was the stimulation in the classroom. The result or consequence for the child is that it is calming to be out of the classroom. He achieved his objective to calm himself by removing himself from the offending stimulus.

For the teacher in the classroom, it is most helpful to figure out what caused the child's sense of being overwhelmed preceding the flight from the classroom. What was the antecedent that led to the behavior of running out of the room? Knowing the antecedent enables us to create effective programming by either removing the antecedent or helping the child to learn to tolerate or process exposure to that stimulus. In many cases, even if we know the antecedent, we cannot prevent it. So, we need to teach the child how to recognize when he is feeling uneasy, how to tell others he is feeling this way and, finally, how to appropriately calm himself down.

TYPES OF MOTIVATION

To effectively work with individuals on the spectrum, it is imperative to understand that, in many cases, they will require different types of motivation than those not on the spectrum require in order to complete certain tasks. Intrinsic motivators that are effective for neurotypical kids are often not enough for the child with ASD. Most are not worried about the social ramifications of not succeeding or of receiving a poor grade. However, some kids on the spectrum do not want to appear, on the outside, to be different than the other kids. Usually, the higher the level of functioning in a child, the more this rings true and the less different a child wants to appear, especially for those who are more extroverted in nature.

Educators ask me all the time if particular behaviors are manipulation or if they are truly the result of legitimate exceptionality. This is a very complex distinction to make, although I find, most of the time, that the undesired behavior is due to spectrum issues and is not motivated by the child's desire to manipulate just to get his way. In school, these kids don't want to appear to be different; they want to be the same as everyone else. They are driven to acting out by the discomfort they are experiencing, in spite of their desire to look like everyone else. Therefore, they act out of control because they are on the spectrum.

Most kids with ASD don't have the same *intrinsic motivation* (i.e. motivation from inside the individual) as neuro-typical kids. Here is an example of intrinsic motivation. On one occasion, my daughter was asleep when I arrived home one evening. When I went to her room to kiss her, I found a note to me that she had secured to her head with a headband. It read, "Please wake me at 6 tomorrow so you can help me study for my math test." She was intrinsically motivated to do well on her test for several reasons: her own satisfaction in doing a good job; her desire to please her parents and teacher; and a friendly competition with one of her close girlfriends, who was also a good student. These types of behaviors wouldn't happen with many children on the spectrum who, for the most part, couldn't care less about a test grade, how their parents feel about it, or how they compare to other kids. A grade is too abstract a motivator for them. They are consumed with meeting more specific needs. They do not have the intrinsic motivation to do well "just because."

Most of the kids I treat for ASD require *extrinsic motivation,* which is motivation that comes from outside the individual. This is the "what's-in-it-for-me?" attitude. Unlike my daughter, who did not receive anything for her good grades (e.g., money, a new game, ice cream, etc.), a child on the spectrum wants to know, "What do I get if I do what you are asking me to do?" They require this extrinsic motivation to inspire them to act.

For example, a typical strategy that parents of kids on the spectrum employ to help with motivation might be, "If you go to therapy today, we can stop at McDonald's on the way home." The child wants to go to McDonald's, so he tolerates the therapy session, which becomes a means-to-an-end. The concern for parents is how to create the extrinsic motivation when they cannot be with the child.

Here is an example of the behavioral contrast between extrinsically and intrinsically motivated kids: I was recently in a fifth-grade classroom where the teacher was giving a lesson on social studies. We had devised a program for a student with autism that tapped into his extrinsic motivators. When the teacher requested that the class read pages 25 to 30 in their textbooks and answer the five questions at the end of the section, 24 students took out their books and began to read; some looked at the length of the reading, some glanced at the questions, but they all read. They were intrinsically motivated. The child with autism took out his book, opened to the five questions, and raised his hand. The teacher went to his desk and he asked, pointing to the questions, "What do I get if I do the five questions?" The teacher replied, "Five minutes of your choice time at the end of the day." The boy asked, "Can I read for my choice time?" The teacher replied, "Yes," and off he went.

It's easy to imagine how that teacher, if she had not understood the need for extrinsic motivation, might have misinterpreted the boy's behavior and actually believed that he was being self-centered, questioning her authority, or just being rude. If she had not been aware of his legitimate exceptionality, her response could have set off an emotional scene or meltdown; instead, her understanding facilitated a calm and effective behavioral response from the child.

ACCOUNTABILITY AND EXECUTIVE FUNCTIONING

This section might have been more aptly named "Understanding Lack of Accountability and Executive Functioning." This is an area in which many of these kids struggle, and it creates a lot of difficulty for parents. It is tied to motivation, to linear thinking, and to social processing.

One common dynamic I see is that, in many situations, children on the spectrum don't perceive a responsibility for their actions. They

EXECUTIVE FUNCTIONING

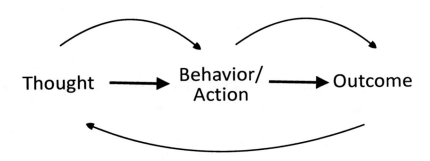

Diagram 8.1 - When someone lacks executive functioning, his thought process is very linear (represented by the straight arrows); that person fails to see the connection between his actions and the results of his actions. When a person is engaged in executive functioning, his thought process (represented by curved arrows) will connect consequences to behavior and will consider the outcome before taking action.

simply don't connect themselves to the outcome that is a direct result of their actions. What they perceive is that, if things went the way they wanted them to, they would never be upset. So, in their world, if you did what they wanted, then they would not be forced to act out. Therefore, it is your fault that they act out.

For example, if you say, "We are going to go to Target at 10:00 a.m.," but at 10:00 a.m. you are unable to go, this might cause a meltdown in which the child becomes destructive and breaks something. From the child's perspective, it is your fault that she broke something. If you had done what you were supposed to do, she would not have had a meltdown and would not have been destructive. Therefore, it was your fault for creating the antecedent rather than her fault for not responsibly managing her reaction. That is how executive functioning difficulties keep children on the spectrum from connecting their actions with the outcome. Thus, executive functioning and accountability are tied together.

Diagram 8.1 illustrates the difference between the actions of someone who lacks executive functioning compared to the actions of someone who is engaging in executive functioning. Basically, executive functioning is the ability to understand cause and effect. If I throw a rock at a window (cause), the window will break (effect); if the window breaks (cause), I am responsible and will have to pay to fix it (effect). The key to executive functioning is considering an outcome and its consequences before engaging in the behavior.

A child might pick up a rock and throw it through a window, unaware that the outcome will be that he will be in trouble. This is an executive functioning issue; the child is unable to project the outcome of the action he is taking (see diagram 8.1). When the child is held accountable for his actions, he becomes very angry because, from his perspective, he feels that no one told him that he would get in trouble. So, he feels he shouldn't be held accountable if he didn't know what the outcome would be.

Kids with executive functioning issues are not able to piece together events and outcomes; they cannot think a situation all the way through, so it is hard for them to connect the dots and see the whole picture, which makes it hard for them to accept responsibility. When they are confronted with the consequences of their actions, they often claim unfairness. They feel it is unfair to be held accountable for an outcome they were unaware would occur.

Remember, these kids are not processing information in the same way as their neuro-typical siblings and friends; they haven't developed mirror neurons and social processing skills. Therefore, they are not watching and learning from the environment or from the experiences of others, and they are not using that information to adjust or develop their behavior. They have to learn each lesson separately, one by one (linearly). They also cannot globalize their experiences because each time is a "new now." We will discuss this concept further in a later section.

As a result of their concrete and linear thinking, children on the spectrum do not apply world knowledge (abstract information) in these situations to aid in their understanding. For example, if they had ever heard a story about a boy who broke a window and got into trouble, they could not apply this information to their own rock and window scenario. They can't connect those two separate events because of their linear thinking.

Most neuro-typical kids don't need to be told that specific acts in which they might engage could have a negative outcome. They are able to *generalize*, that is, learn from one experience and apply it to another. For example, if they are told that taking a gun to school is not allowed, then, they will realize that taking a knife to school isn't a good idea, either. They can deduce that, in general, weapons are not allowed at school, and then draw the appropriate conclusion. In many cases, kids with autism are unable to piece those two ideas together. As parents, educators, and therapists, it is impossible for us to know what they are thinking all the time in order to stay one step ahead of them, warning them in advance about all of the possible consequences of each of their choices.

One of my young clients, angry over the fact that school was starting, sent an email to his principal, stating that if school started on the day it was scheduled to do so, that he would blow up the building. The school principal (whom I happened to know) contacted me and asked if I thought he might take any such action. I knew this student and knew that there was zero chance of this happening. He ended up getting suspended from school, but he didn't understand what he had done. In his mind, if school hadn't been scheduled to start, there wouldn't have been a problem. He didn't understand the ramifications of his actions. He was unable to see the serious nature of his actions on a social level; he did not understand the "no tolerance policy" that schools follow today.

"QUIRKY" BEHAVIOR

Quirky is an adjective that describes the appearance of many of these kids—they just appear to be odd. Imagine a young man with a 120+ IQ score, someone who can carry on a very intelligent conversation about meaningful topics, but who wears his shirts backwards. As a younger child, he had seen a cartoon character running, and to this day he puts his head down and sticks his arms straight out behind him when he runs. He can tell you the names of all the Pokeman characters, as well as their lineage, their special powers, and the best way to catch them. He can beat almost any videogame in a matter of days, but he won't go to the videogame store and conduct a transaction with the clerk behind the counter because he is uncomfortable with the unknown in the situation. These kids often appear just a bit different from everyone else.

UNDERSTANDING THE SELF-RESTRICTIVE PERSPECTIVE

I regularly see a pattern of behavior that I call a *self-restrictive perspective*. Since kids on the spectrum lack the intrinsic motivation to do things just because, it is typical that something that they are required to do, like homework, makes no sense in their world. They see school as the place for schoolwork and home as the place for relaxing. Doing homework just because it is what is expected of them makes no sense to them at all.

In their world, homework is "not right, not fair." So, avoiding homework is not wrong, it is simply not doing something that is not right to begin with. Because they do not learn in a dynamic, social manner (i.e., from watching others, generalizing concepts, and using executive functioning to piece together outcomes or project into the future), kids with ASD have no data to support the reason to do homework. By not doing it, they are simply getting out of something they think they should not have to do in the first place.

This pattern of thinking often results in what app~~~~ or, simply, not tracking on reality. It can appear ~~~~ the child just doesn't get it. And that's true, the ~~~~ it—but that's not a value judgment, it's a fact ~~~~ different processing system. Of course, simpl~~~~ there is a neurological underpinning doesn't nec~~~~ to accept or tolerate the resulting behavior in a family member, especially if that behavior takes the form of his truth—the truth as he sees it, which is not the same as the rest of the world sees it.

As a parent or other authority figure, dealing with this type of thinking and its resulting behavior is frustrating and complex. Knowing what the end result of the child's choice is likely to be is what makes the situation so debilitating to parents. Saying to the child, "Look at Uncle Bob; he lives in grandma's basement because he was not able to graduate from high school," falls on deaf ears. The child with autism thinks, "But, I am not Uncle Bob." Kids without ASD would be able to draw a comparison and say, "I don't want to be like that," and then make the appropriate choices.

For a parent, in the heat of the moment the situation can feel hopeless, as if there is no way to reasonably parent such a self-centered, stubborn, unmotivated individual. I'm sure this can escalate in many situations (in volume if nothing else). Understanding your child's executive functioning, motivation, and perspective will give you the groundwork you need to build a successful strategy for intervention.

CHAPTER 9

ANXIETY AND CONTROL

For individuals on the spectrum, life is all about control. They want to control everything around them in order to feel more grounded and less anxious.

The tendency to reduce anxiety by controlling the environment is common to all of us. Everyone does it, not just those on the spectrum. We have all encountered anxious feelings in our lives when we are dealing with a new school, a new job, a move to a new town, etc. The more we know about what is going on around us and what the expectations are, the less stress we feel. In this context, our perception is that control equals safety.

Have you ever had a day when everything went exactly the way you wanted it to, down to the last detail? No. We rarely, if ever, have days like this, however, most neuro-typical individuals adapt. This morning, I didn't plan on getting stuck in traffic, but I did. Even a minor change, like a detour on your way to work, is a change, something not in your plan.

UNDERSTANDING THE NEED TO CONTROL IN ORDER TO REDUCE ANXIETY

For individuals on the spectrum, life is all about control. They want to control everything around them in order to feel more grounded and less anxious. For them, the unknown is extremely unpleasant, while for those of us not on the spectrum, this can be what makes life exciting. Individuals with autism seem to obsess and worry about areas in their lives that they do not have any control over, like the weather. Because of this, they may feel that things are out of their control most of the time.

As children, they often express their need to control by developing an intense interest in their physical environment. For example, a child may focus on the consistent (not necessarily neat) appearance of his bedroom. If you move a pen marker in that room, he will come in and straighten it out and he'll probably be angry about it, because his room is the safest place for him, and he wants it to always be the same. Home is the safest place; it is where these children have the most control and the most freedom to be themselves. Things that are not negotiable in other arenas of life tend to be more flexible at home.

Individuals on the spectrum focus on the consistencies in the physical environment to reduce anxiety. The young man who came into therapy because the couch was moved to make room for the Christmas tree was 17 years old. It actually took three therapy sessions to deal with the couch moving two feet! As is the case in therapy, in the process of working through that issue, that young man began to create interconnectivity and to develop flexibility and some coping skills.

There are three times per year when I see anxiety levels peak, not for everyone on the spectrum, but for most: the beginning of the school year, the end of the school year, and the holiday season.

The holiday season is a time of year that most people really enjoy and get excited about, especially children. It is part of the excitement to see and participate in changes in the environment: stringing lights; decorating a Christmas tree; playing seasonal music; attending parties. During this time, routines at school and at home change. We enjoy all of the preparations for the big event to come. The anticipation is part of the fun for children waiting for Christmas morning; the most exciting part for the kids is opening their new toys. Another bonus is that they have school recess for a couple of weeks. Wow, how can you beat that, new toys and no school. They can hardly wait! Ask a teacher what it's like at school the last couple of days before Christmas break. Do you think anyone accomplishes much during this time?

What about for children on the spectrum? How do you think that they view all the change around the holidays? Again, apply my rule of thumb—whatever makes most individuals excited and feel positive anxiety makes those on the spectrum feel the opposite. They are usually not happy about the upcoming holiday season with all the changes heading their way. They are not excited about the lights, the tree, the decorations, or the music. In many cases, they do not want school to end because it is so familiar and structured (usually). They do not want unknown gifts under a tree that should not be there. All of this activity creates a great deal of anxiety for children with autism as changes in their regular routine begin to become apparent.

FIXATIONS

Fixations are also an attempt to control. Becoming fixated on something and using that to escape into your own world is one way of gaining control. Here's an example of a little boy who demonstrates a level of control that is astounding. He's one of the neatest kids I've ever worked with; he assembled a complex train set in about an hour and a half. His dad had tried to follow the box directions to no avail, spending 2½ hours the night before, until he finally gave up. The dad couldn't figure out how to assemble the train set with the help of directions; his son, who has autism, put it together intuitively in an hour and a half! The reason I tell you this story is to illustrate that the world created by the train set is a world that makes sense to this little boy. This is a world that is calming to him; he has control of it. What happens if you move one of those tracks? Now we have a meltdown, now we have a problem, because this is a place he can go where he feels safe, where he feels like he has control, and where things make sense to him.

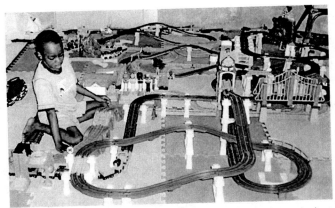

This little boy intuitively assembled a complex train set in just over an hour. Photograph courtesy of Stella Danso

When this little boy gets a chance during the day or during the evening to think about something, what do you suppose he thinks about? That train set. Not what his buddies are doing, not what the other kids are doing; the train set is what he's focusing on.

I worked with a little boy whom I would consider a map savant. He could not wait to get home from school so he could study his maps. It's amazing how children with autism can control their brains if they're thinking about something they like, something that comforts them.

If these little boys were fixated on football, they would potentially be more social because football is an interest many kids have in common. Often, children on the spectrum have special interests that are unusual, which serves to isolate them and, depending on what the fixation is, may even make them appear odd to the rest of the world. Remember, they do not have a social filter to evaluate the coolness factor of their fixations. As a result of not having this filter, they are not able to accurately access whether or not everyone else likes what they are focused on, or if they should talk about it with their peers.

For example, I recently worked with a young man who was obsessed with the color pink. He did not see that no other boys in the fifth grade liked the color pink, nor did he understand that even though he liked pink he should not announce it to his whole class, lest he not fit in. In therapy, we discussed the possibility that he might not even say that he liked a different color, but this became further complicated by the fact that he did not want to lie by saying his favorite color was something other than pink.

Those not on the spectrum might relate to this type of anxiety by thinking about it this way: What if you had no idea what you would be doing for work each day, who your boss would be, where you would be working, or what would be expected of you? Can you imagine going to bed each night and trying to relax? Living under those conditions would be very stressful. Those of us not on the spectrum may like consistency in our lives on many levels, but we are flexible enough to handle the subtle changes without giving them any thought. The difference between us and children with autism is that we can move on from those changes comfortably, whereas they can't. They get stuck. Individuals with autism need to learn to accept life for what it is—unpredictable, changing, and abstract.

From a therapeutic standpoint, we want to address the need to control by helping the child develop give and take, i.e., develop a little flexibility. It's okay to like maps, but let's also get outside a little bit and shoot some baskets. As I have mentioned, I have two goals therapeutically: that the kids are happy and that they are functional. Being functional means being able to go outside and shoot baskets, being able to interact with the world, and being able to rebound (emotionally, not literally) quickly when an unplanned event occurs. That's it; that's all I'm trying to do. I want these individuals to understand and accept their autism and to learn to enhance and develop their skills in order to be functional in a social world.

USING ROUTINES TO CONTROL

Creating a very structured, consistent routine is another way that individuals with ASD control the environment in order to handle stressful situations. In the movie *Rain Man*, Judge Wapner was on television every day at 4:30 p.m. and the character Raymond needed to watch it. Raymond made sense of the world around him by controlling his day and making it consistent; watching Judge Wapner was a critical part of that routine. It would create a great deal of anxiety if he could not watch his regularly scheduled program. Just like it did for Raymond, changing a routine for a child with autism decreases predictability, which increases anxiety. Routines help to manage anxiety by translating an otherwise chaotic world into black and white.

The 8-year-old map savant would do something very interesting while he was traveling by car in order to feel like he had control over the amount of time and distance he was traveling. His routine, while he traveled, was to memorize all the exit signs for each city and count the mile markers. Therefore, at each mile marker he would know exactly how far it would be until they reached the next exit and the final destination. In performing this task, he was able to relieve stress and anxiety by controlling the environment around him, which made the trip very black and white in his head. His mother reported that his older sister would often ask how far along they were, and his mother would simply ask him how many more miles. He would always know exactly how far they were from their final destination: "52 miles to exit 118, Mom, and then it is 8 miles north from there."

As a general rule, these kids feel safer and function better with a consistent routine, whether they create it or someone creates it for them. The same is true for having strong boundaries, which provide these kids with the structure they need to succeed, while at the same time reducing anxiety. Much more about boundaries is discussed in the following chapters.

FIGHTING FOR CONTROL

Children with autism have an incredible aversion to doing things that they do not want to do. That aversion is magnified by their black and white, all-or-none thinking; as a result, they spend a lot of time making sure that the boundaries and rules that have been set in place are still in effect, or fighting against those rules in order to do only what they want to do. Demanding control is an effort to manage their anxiety.

They get stuck not wanting to do something, and they will try anything to find a way around it, unable to realize how they only prolong their own discomfort. For example, if they just did their homework, it might only take 20 minutes, but instead they suffer for three hours to try to get out of 20 minutes of work. Once again, we see this type of behavior as a result of a self-restricting perspective. Behaviorally, it looks like these children on the spectrum will say or do anything to avoid doing what they don't want to do. They may even contradict themselves, change directions or tactics midstream, or lie— all because they are mentally tied in a knot, stuck not wanting to do something.

If I ask my children to take out the garbage, I can explain that it will take two minutes to do it, and then they can play for the rest of the day. They think about it, and they decide that they will get the chore over with, even though they don't want to do it.

A child stuck in his self-restrictive perspective may argue with you for one hour about doing a two-minute chore. Children on the spectrum get cognitively stuck not wanting to do the chore, hoping for the time when they can win the argument and won't have to do what they don't want to do. If this has worked even once in the past, they will try harder to win. This, again, is black and white, all-or-none thinking. If it has worked before, why won't it work today?

To complicate matters further, a child on the spectrum may not have the social understanding to piece together related concepts that would support them doing what they don't want to do. For example, when asked to clean a toilet, they think, "Why should I clean the toilet, it's not my house!" They are not able to cognitively assess the fact that everyone else in the house does chores to support the household, too. So, the rule that we do chores as part of being family participants does not make sense to them.

More than once, I have heard a child say to me or his parent, "Why are you ruining my life?" From their ASD perspective, these kids cannot understand why we would intentionally make painful demands or put uncomfortable boundaries on them—boundaries that cause aggravation and frustration, and tap into the wellspring of pain that has developed inside them.

One crucial concept I try to teach the kids in my care is that, in life, we all have to do things we don't want to do. Everyone does—not just adults, but kids, too—whether you are neuro-typical or on the spectrum. The kids I treat struggle with social competency in a socially based society. Living in our society requires a lot of doing what they don't want to do, and often results in anger and frustration. I will often say, "You don't have to like it, you just have to do it."

An ASD child often lacks intrinsic motivation, and therefore needs healthy and firm boundaries to guide her behavior. Strong boundaries work because they act as extrinsic motivation. To get my intrinsically motivated social daughter to brush her teeth, all I have to do is suggest that if she doesn't brush her teeth, her breath will stink. She can take it from there, immediately deducing that brushing her teeth will give her fresh breath and a nice smile, and that is a good thing to her; she can then follow through.

For a child on the spectrum, a parent might explain in painful detail the disagreeable consequences of not brushing one's teeth—bad breath, rotting teeth, painful and expensive dentistry—and the child most likely will not brush his teeth anyway. If the boundary is set up so that if he does not brush his teeth, he will lose time on the computer (something most children dearly love), then he may consent to brushing his teeth. This boundary will probably need to be reinforced over and over again. This same routine might be required for days and days on end to be effective—if it is ever effective!

Many parents tell me it is such hard work to stay on top of each little thing a child must do, like brushing teeth. These parents realize that if they are not standing in the bathroom each time the child brushes, he will stand at the sink with the water running, wet the toothbrush, and claim to have brushed his teeth. All the child on the spectrum knows is that if he can avoid doing it now, he can avoid the discomfort. It is incredibly demanding as parents, because if we let up even once, we may set the learning curve back to zero again. Kids on the spectrum require structured parenting and consistent boundaries, times 10.

As parents, educators, and therapists caring for these children, we have a constant battle with them as they experience frustration, and the resulting anger, and try to control the world around them to manage their discomfort. This battle never ends; we can never let up, because the minute we do, they will find the opening. This is not to say that a child on the spectrum can never learn, but it is much more difficult for them; it is times 10. A parent recently said to me that it is like a constant tug of war and if she lets go even a little bit, her child takes the rope.

CONTROL WITH STIMMING BEHAVIORS

As mentioned in Chapter 4, How Autism Develops, when children on the spectrum perform continuous, repetitive behavior for the purpose of calming down, it is called self-stimulatory behavior or stimming; it is their attempt to control themselves. Stimming consists of motor movements, such as flapping or spinning, or looking at objects for long periods of time, such as the spinning of wheels on a toy car. Some individuals have told me that they just feel like they have to do it, or that they cannot stop it from happening. Stimming gives the individual some level of control over his own psychological state.

Consider the inhibitory/excitatory neurons shown in Diagram 4.1 in Chapter 4. Stimming fills the neurological gap; it feels good, or relaxing, to the individual because it allows the brain to reach the point where it can return to homeostasis. The behavior also may serve to tune out an environment that is too stimulating or does not make sense.

There are a number of common behaviors seen in children with autism that arise from the individual's drive to control the environment and/or to calm down. Here are some common examples:

- Flapping hands (especially when excited or stimulated)
- Spinning, balancing, or toe walking
- Exhibiting a preoccupation with hand movement
- Showing aggressiveness towards others
- Throwing tantrums
- Showing lack of interest in typical toys (e.g., prefers kitchen tools, toothbrush); turns toy car over and spins wheels for extended periods of time
- Obsessive attachment to objects (yellow banana, toothbrush)
- Spinning objects
- Exhibiting sustained odd play
- Exhibiting an obsession with patterns
- Repeating behavior (watching opening of movie or playing jingle on computer over and over)
- Lining up things (especially toy cars, can be any object, e.g., brooms)
- Exhibiting self-injurious behaviors
- Self-regulating/soothing

ANXIETY AND OBSESSIVE TENDENCIES/OCD TENDENCIES

Those who develop obsessive tendencies are compulsively attempting to control their environment through their own behavior. Refer to Chapter 6, Spectrum Development, for a detailed discussion on the development of obsessive tendencies and OCD as a coping mechanism for anxiety.

CHAPTER 10

UNDERSTANDING AUTISM AS A SOCIAL DISABILITY

For both parents and teachers, balancing the need to make
adjustments in expectations and the need to hold these kids
accountable so they can learn to function in society is tricky.

*I*t is easy to see that a concrete, black and white, linear way of processing information in order to analyze and interpret any social situation cannot be effective in complex, ever-changing interactions. Again, in the brain of a child with ASD, the allocation of resources is devoted to processing the sensory environment, not necessarily to processing the social environment. So, unlike neuro-typical children, children on the spectrum are not building a repertoire of social skills as they develop. With all of these factors working against them, it becomes increasingly clear why they have a social disability and why it is one of their main issues; this impacts every other area of the individual's life.

SOCIAL COMPLEXITY, VULNERABILITY, AND THE NEED TO FIT IN

Public speaking (social phobia) is often touted as the number one phobia in the world. Social phobia is the fear of being evaluated negatively in social situations. Typically, social phobia begins in childhood or adolescence. Individuals on the spectrum experience social phobia, just times 10. Remember the discussion of sitting in traffic and becoming aware of someone looking at you? Imagine having that feeling times 10! It would make you want to jump right out of your skin.

The most complex interchange that takes place for human beings is the social interaction. Nothing in a social interaction is exactly the same twice. If we are neuro-typical, there are many subtle nuances to our interactions that, once experienced, become hardwired into our brains and automatically provide us with feedback regarding a current interaction—that's interconnectivity at work. For those of us not on the spectrum, we are constantly adapting and changing our expectations and behavior. We use executive functioning to learn from past experiences. It is the proverbial, "I will never say or do that again!" scenario. People on the spectrum may need to experience the same discomfort 10 times to learn the lesson, if they ever learn it.

Social behavior is incredibly complicated, and our ability to recognize and interpret it is directly related to our processing of incoming information. When you're at a party and someone tells a joke and you don't get it, what do you do? Laugh, right? You're not going to say, "Wait! I'm sorry. I know this is the third one, but I really don't get this one either—can someone please explain it to me?" We don't expose ourselves by admitting that we don't understand, and neither do kids on the spectrum.

In the classroom, teachers will often tell kids on the spectrum to just raise their hand and ask a question if they don't understand. As if it is that simple. That's a bit like asking the lamb to volunteer to go to slaughter. Many healthy, neuro-typical individuals won't open themselves up that way, why would a child on the spectrum, who already suffers from anxiety and other social issues, want to create a situation that is drawing more attention to himself? He won't. In fact, many individuals on the spectrum work very hard to fly under the radar, to slip between the cracks; they often become very good at imitating others in order to go unnoticed or to better navigate the social environment and appear to fit in.

For parents or teachers, balancing the need to make adjustments in our expectations and the need to hold these kids accountable so they can learn to function in society is tricky. There are true exceptionalities that need accommodation, but my experience is also that the parents who create structure, clarify expectations, and hold firm to their boundaries raise kids who perform better and feel better, both as children and as adults. Kids need to learn to fit in to the degree that allows them to function effectively in a social world. For those who lack the ability to discern many things on their own, strict guidelines will help them achieve that.

FALLING BETWEEN THE CRACKS

Given the chance, kids on the spectrum would not force themselves to become independent and functional. Instead, they would take every opportunity to avoid what's difficult for them in the moment.

Many learn to fly under the radar by behaving as if they understand how to work the system, thus escaping scrutiny, but not actually functioning within the system as it is established. They find ways to avoid their issues, rather than finding functional ways to compensate, like learning the skill, or self- advocating. Eventually, this backfires. For example, recently I worked with a child whose mother and teachers had created a system that would enable him to manage his homework effectively. He had a folder that held all of his assignments. Both the uncompleted and completed assignments were to be kept in it. At the end of the school day, all he had to do was bring the folder home, and he would have his homework assignments. This would keep him organized.

Instead, to avoid being punished for assignments that weren't completed, he devised a plan to get out of doing what he did not want to do. He began to pull all the assignments out of the folder at the end of the day and stuff them into his locker, telling his mom that everything was done, and telling the teachers that the assignments were left at home. By playing both ends against the middle, he escaped scrutiny in the short term. Of course, this strategy was ineffective for the long term.

Facing the issues head on and discovering how to cope opens up endless possibilities for the future. Children on the spectrum are often very bright and talented young people who have limitless potential once they harness their talents and learn to tow the line.

CLASSROOM COPS/PEER INTERACTIONS

Those of us who are neuro-typical may not even recognize the social challenges we face everyday. We operate at the next level, naturally and automatically incorporating the information we are learning into our social experience database. For example, we say that men and women do not interact on the same level, but many of us are able to traverse that difference effectively without too much conscious effort. Not so for kids with ASD. A lot of these kids have to be taught specifically to maneuver the social landscape.

For example, they have to be taught not to be the "classroom police." The teacher will ask, "Who did that?" and the child with ASD will say, "Tim did." All the rest of the kids in the classroom are thinking, "Why would you say something like that? Why would you turn Tim in?" The child on the spectrum only sees the black and white facts and simply restates those facts, unaware that he is committing "social suicide," as one teacher put it. The problem for some individuals on the spectrum is that they are so fixated on the rules that a situation where someone is not following the rules creates a great deal of anxiety for them.

The situation can be even more complex. You say to these kids, "You really shouldn't turn your friends in. You don't narc on your friends," and then a circumstance arises where it is appropriate to tell on their friends, yet they are not able to make that leap. Do you tell on your friends or do you not? Their black and white thinking doesn't allow them to put the concept of telling on their friends in both categories. Their rigid thinking dictates that either you do it all the time, or you never do it.

I met a young man who had been hanging out with the wrong group of friends. These friends planned to vandalize a school that was under construction. There was a porta-potty on the grounds, and when they arrived at the site, the young man needed to use it. While his so-called friends are vandalizing the school, he's in the bathroom—he didn't even know what was happening. Of course, then the police show up. When he comes out of the porta-potty, the school is vandalized and the cops see his friends running away. This young man claims, "Well I didn't do anything, I was in the toilet." What do all his so-called friends say? They claim that he did it.

So, now he's in my office and we're discussing the situation. I tell him, "You've got to tell me what happened." He says, "Well, you don't narc on your friends." I try to explain to him that he needs to understand that all of these friends are turning him in—he will pay the consequences for something that he didn't do. "No, they wouldn't do that," he says. He was unable to see that his friends could have a different perspective than he does. He believes he is doing the right, ethical thing. He thinks, "I am doing what I am supposed to do, which is not telling on my friends, and since I wouldn't do it to them, they wouldn't do it to me." This is the essence of not having an intact theory of mind—the belief that another individual thinks in the same way and has the same perspective as you do. The individual with this issue is unable to see things from any other perspective but his own, and he assumes you see things that way, too.

This young man could have been in a great deal of trouble. It took a lot of convincing on my part to get him to tell me the truth so I could talk to the lawyer to make sure that he didn't get all the blame pinned on him. That's the difficulty for these kids as they grow up environment is so complex, and their approach is so blac̓ That disconnect can create some big difficulties in their lives.

One of the smartest kids with whom I've ever worked (he earned a score of 32 on his ACT exam, the highest in his entire high school) is now attending a prestigious technical institute, studying to be a chemical engineer. One day, he was in my office telling me how he'd just been fired from his job bringing the carts in at the grocery store. As he recounted his story, he described that he had been fired because he took the time cards and went to the supervisor with the names of everybody who was taking too long for breaks. The kid with the highest ACT score in his high school got fired from his job at the grocery store for saying, "Hey, Tom had a break two minutes too long yesterday. As the supervisor, I think you should know that." How did that go over with his peers at work? Not well at all. His boss asked him to stop doing this, but he couldn't. He was doing what he thought was right, following the rules and reporting those who did not. He was doing a grown-up version of classroom police. Do you suppose he was popular?

If I instructed any of my daughters to tell on their classmates, they would not do it. I could not pay them to do this. Why wouldn't they do it? Because of the social implications of being a tattletale. This young man *will* be a chemical engineer—but he also got fired from the grocery store for reading the time cards of his coworkers. That is one of the best ways that I can describe autism—that contradiction between high intelligence/mental ability and tremendous social disability. That is the crux of the issue for people on the spectrum.

As they get older, many individuals with autism do want to fit in socially (especially those who are extroverted). One client told me, "I can see how much fun a social interaction can be, but it is very hard and makes me very nervous to be in one." Again, this is the trap in which higher functioning individuals on the spectrum find themselves. Autism is a social disability. The smartest individual (on paper) in his high school was fired for doing something I could not pay my 8-year-old to do.

THE SOCIAL IMPACT OF HONESTY, LYING, AND RULE FOLLOWING

I am often asked if kids on the spectrum can lie. Some professionals believe that they cannot lie. Some individuals on the spectrum can lie, and do, and it is usually to avoid doing something uncomfortable. I have seen kids lie even when all the evidence has caught them red-handed, because they believed that I could not know that they were lying.

One child summed this up well. He told me that if he told the truth right away he was caught right away, with no chance to get off the hook for what he did. If he lied, he had a chance to get away with it. So, he would lie even though he knew that he would get into twice the trouble for doing so.

The boy who would hide his homework in his locker said that he lied because there was a chance to get away with it. Kids on the spectrum can lie as an attempt to avoid the discomfort of doing something that is painful for them or of doing something that challenges their world. I have to ask myself, how painful must something be if even a slim chance of success at lying to avoid it is worth risking the chance of getting caught for twice the punishment?

Individuals on the spectrum are skilled at remembering details, and this actually works against them when it comes to lying. They can remember when they lied in the past and got away with it. Their black and white thinking causes them to believe that it could happen today just as it did five years ago. They do not use executive functioning to evaluate all the times they were caught, nor do they use that data to conclude that it is not worth it to try to lie.

The whole concept of lying becomes even more perverse when we try to explain the white lie to a black and white, concrete-thinking child on the spectrum. Do I lie or tell the truth? Lying is bad, right? We never lie. When your spouse asks you what you think of her new shirt, haircut, etc., what do you say?

Imagine the potential social implications if we don't teach our kids about white lies. Individuals on the spectrum usually struggle in this area and are prone to "tell it like it is," which may appear socially awkward or rude. If I ask them, "Do you like my shirt?" and they don't, they will say, "No, I do not like blue." Those of us with good social skills wonder why someone would say something potentially offensive like that. The spectrum child is thinking, "Why would you ask me if you didn't want to know what I really thought?" They simply do not have typical social filters to guide their communications. The point is, in some cases a white lie is appropriate.

Another example of the socially acceptable white lie is small talk. If I get home at night and my neighbor Terry is outside when I pull in my driveway, I will say, "Hi, Terry, how is it going?" What does he say? "Good, Tim, how are you?" No matter what I am feeling, I reply "Good, Terry, thanks," and exit the exchange with a smile. If I said, "Oh, Terry, my day was horrible, the economy is bad, some guy cut me off in traffic, and my computer bombed out," and go on with the sordid details of my day, what will Terry probably do when he sees me coming the next night? Run into his garage and close the door! White lies are commonly accepted as a social standard in situations like this where small talk is appropriate. However, someone on the spectrum, who thinks in concrete, black and white terms, does not understand the social subtleties of the white lie.

On the flip side, one advantage to the linear thinking of children on the spectrum is that they are, for the most part, rule followers. When they learn a rule, they learn it well. However, sometimes they learn it too well. They get stuck, and are therefore unable to make an exception, or to adjust their initial understanding of a concept. This is the root of the problem that causes children on the spectrum to become the classroom police and tell on anyone who is breaking a rule.

STORYTELLING—THE TALL TALE

Storytelling is another interesting phenomenon that arises as a result of inadequate social filters and the need to fit in and make conversation. By storytelling, I mean those times when a story becomes far fetched to the point of being unbelievable. I heard about a young lady who told her mother she almost drowned and was saved by a lifeguard at the pool. Her father, who was with her at the time, was totally shocked because he knew nothing of the situation. My guess is that it didn't really happen. Part of the challenge for those on the spectrum is that they tell these stories within the framework of all-or-none thinking and they are unable to see how egregious the story is.

There are a number of reasons that these kids tell these types of tall tales. In some cases, I think it is a way to enter a conversation or to impress others, however, usually the story lacks any social filter to make sense to people. I have also seen how a child might use storytelling to make a point about someone who, in the child's mind, had wronged him somehow. For example, I had a client who fabricated a story about being attacked at the bus stop because a teacher from the school did not walk him to the bus when he wanted her to. As a result, he blamed her for the alleged attack. The problem is that stories like these are so absurd that they do not make sense. I see this frequently, and it is one of the reasons I encourage parents to attend therapy sessions with their child. I can usually tell, with a quick glance at the parent, if the story has validity, if it is grossly exaggerated, or if it is entirely made up. I once suggested to one of my clients that he learn to play chess; he came back the next week and told me that he could beat the computer chess game on the master level. That was obviously a tall tale.

Children may tell these stories to gain attention from others, because they do not have the social skills to do it naturally. They may fake an illness to gain attention from peers at school; unfortunately, they often fake a serious illness, like brain cancer for instance. The first time someone attempts this type of storytelling, he may attract an abundance of attention, however, as you can imagine, if he attempts it again, it could have serious social consequences.

My approach in dealing with this issue is to break the story down and address each fact in the narrative, using logic and linear thinking. Often, the child will admit that the pieces of the story just do not fit. Trying to understand the motivation behind the storytelling is an important factor in helping these kids overcome this type of lying.

WHAT A SOCIAL DISABILITY LOOKS LIKE

When I was in graduate school and saw my first client with autism, my supervisor said, "Tim, you need to understand that you are not going to feel the same social connectivity as you do with the rest of your clients. You have to understand that when you are dealing with children on the spectrum, you may not get that warm smile all the time. It isn't that the children don't love; they have a social disability."

In the fictional *Star Trek*, the character named Mr. Spock is a black and white thinker; he is capable of love, but has trouble showing it. He thinks in numbers and constantly analyzes data, even if the data involves human emotions and human life. He often argues that Captain Kirk's decisions are illogical. The difficulty Kirk has with Spock is a result of the clash between emotional thinking and linear thinking.

For example, Kirk would risk the lives of everyone on the spaceship in order to save two people trapped on the planet. Spock does not see this as a logical decision. "Why would you leave us in the gravitational pull of this planet that could destroy us in a half hour, when there are only two people down there to save and there are 375 people on the ship? Let's get out of here." Kirk insists, "No, we have to try and save them." Spock, incredulous, asks, "You're going to risk 375 lives instead of just leaving? You're going to try and rescue these two? That's illogical." And, of course, Kirk replies, "Yes, I am."

Spock is a linear thinker who does care for other people, but who does not show it emotionally; he has a different perspective. His view is not wrong, it's just not the social norm, and therefore it is different than what most people experience. Although he appears very cold and unemotional, he demonstrates that he does care because, in the end, he sacrifices his own life to save the spaceship. Based on his nonsocial behavior, I would conclude (if he wasn't a Vulcan) that Mr. Spock is on the spectrum.

UNCERTAINTY IN SOCIAL SITUATIONS

The uncertainty of even the simplest social interactions stresses the system of those on the spectrum. Think about something as basic as making a phone call or answering the phone. These activities can provoke anxiety for individuals with ASD because of the unknown. You are never sure who will be at the other end of the line, whether you make the call or receive it, and you are never sure what that person is going to say. I have had clients with ASD tell me that someone called them and that this was frustrating to them because they did not know they were going to get the call. They would actually benefit from receiving a letter in the mail stating the time and date of the phone call that they were going to receive, along with information about who was calling and why. This would take an experience that is usually gray and make it black and white, enabling the individual with ASD to process it without getting nervous.

I remember working with a young adult many years ago. I wanted to find a social group for him, and after many phone calls I found one that I thought might fit. It was actually a group for cognitively delayed adults, because there were no groups for autism 15 years ago. I called their main office to lay some advance groundwork, and spoke with the secretary. I explained that a young man named Sam would be calling, that he had autism and may struggle a little bit with his conversation with her. She was very nice and said that she would be able to help him out during the conversation. I had all the details of the group set up, but I wanted Sam to call for himself.

Sam was nervous about the call and we literally spent three therapy sessions practicing the phone call to the secretary to set up his participation in the group. Sam came to my office every week with a new set of questions that we would practice. What if she says this, what if she says that, etc? What I found interesting is that Sam had no problems in our sessions answering any questions or comments I made during our practice phone calls, he was just very nervous about the unknown.

Finally, I convinced Sam to call. When he called, the secretary answered and said, "Could you please hold?" Well, guess what? We did not practice that one! He immediately shut down and hung up. He could not process this unexpected scenario. He was upset because he was ready to talk and he thought it was rude of her to put him on hold! It took me weeks to get him to call again. What seems to neuro-typical individuals to be a simple phone call is a complex social interaction full of anxiety about the unknown for those on the spectrum. To Sam, social interactions feel like a treacherous minefield that might blow up at any time!

THE PERVASIVE IMPACT OF SOCIAL DEFICITS

What is so difficult about treatment for those with ASD is that the very thing they come to therapy to address is what may prevent them from coming in the first place. They come because they need to increase their social ability which, by the very nature of autism, is something that is painfully uncomfortable for them. So, in order to continue with therapy, they must constantly overcome their discomfort just to get to their sessions.

Think about the frustration for these individuals living in a social world. Imagine wanting to be a rock climber yet being afraid of heights or wanting to be a surgeon and being averse to the sight of blood. For individuals with autism, their issues not only affect their careers, they affect their entire lives. You would not necessarily struggle in life as a whole if you were a rock climber afraid of heights or a surgeon afraid of blood. Your difficulty would be limited to that one single area of your life and you could still be functional, engage in a different hobby, or do something else for a living. It is very challenging to function in life when you are socially deficient. Autistic social deficiency has a global, pervasive impact on the lives of these individuals.

THE SOCIAL IMPACT OF COMMUNICATION DIFFICULTIES

There are a number of issues related to communication for individuals on the spectrum. First, many individuals with ASD tell me that they experience frustration and difficulty in communicating their thoughts. They will often say that they are trying to "say the right thing" or that they are looking for the perfect answer, when there isn't one. They will say that they are waiting for the right time to talk, when there is no right time. This thinking fits the concrete, black and white model of an ASD individual, and can also create very awkward social interactions.

I worked with one adult client who was attempting to articulate his social and communication challenges to me. He did not comprehend why other people could not intuitively understand what he was thinking. Even though he did not show any nonverbal behavior that would help others to understand what he was thinking, he still believed that people should just automatically, intuitively know his thoughts and feelings.

To explain how clear he would like communication to be, he told me about a commercial with Jerry Seinfeld and Bill Gates. In the commercial Jerry says to Bill, "If it's 'yes' just give me a sign." Then, Bill makes a specific physical move to give Jerry the clear signal he is looking for. My client felt that that kind of clear, blatant signal would make communication much easier for him.

Many individuals with ASD describe their processing difficulties by saying to me, "I can either listen to you or look at you, which would you like me to do?" For some individuals on the spectrum, processing visual and auditory stimulation are both cognitive tasks, rendering it nearly impossible to do both at the same time. It can be very distracting to talk with someone who is looking away from you; the natural reaction is to look where they are looking to see if you are missing something. More importantly, due to our social norms, the inability to make eye contact may well be interpreted as disrespect. As you can imagine, this might create social misunderstandings, especially with authority figures.

Since individuals on the spectrum do not develop mirror neurons in the same fashion as those without autism do, another issue that arises is that they do not display empathy during social interactions. Totally missing important social cues, they appear unable to care (ala Mr. Spock), although they are capable of caring as much as their neuro-typical friends.

One of the most difficult social issues that arises is the lack of social reciprocity. Individuals on the spectrum want to talk about what they want to talk about, without worrying about another person's perspective, or the reciprocity that we expect in conversations. As a result, they often appear rude and self-centered.

CHAPTER 11

COPING WITH ANGER

Anger is a familiar emotion for children on the spectrum;
they must live in a world not designed or built for them.

While individuals with autism feel a full range of emotions just like anyone else, for them, anger is typically the most highly developed emotion; it is anger that is most easily communicated to the outside world. Emotions like love and sadness are much more difficult to express.

Imagine living a life that you perceive never goes the way you want it to. EVER. That would make me feel angry. Many of these kids want to stay home and play videogames, eat their favorite foods, and isolate themselves from the painful social interactions they are forced into by daily living. As parents and therapists, we are constantly working against those desires—working to help these children develop their social skills and their ability to function in the world. We are constantly forcing them to do what they don't want to do, what in some cases may actually be painful for them to do. We are forcing them to participate and engage in life. That can produce a lot of anger.

Other kids can go along with the flow. At my house, when we are out of my kids' favorite cereal, they might be upset for a minute, but they will be over it before they finish eating breakfast. For children with ASD, not having their favorite cereal could ruin their entire day. Whenever one small thing does not go the way they want it to, they could be angry and upset and stuck there, unable to move past the offending incident. That's their linear thinking at work.

Over time, incidents like this build up into a wellspring of anger and resentment toward a world that is not fair. As I illustrated in Diagram 7.1, individuals with ASD see everything as black and white; something is either right, or it is wrong—there is no in-between. When something is not 100% fair, it is unfair. That puts a lot more of life in the unfair category.

This issue of fairness comes up often. As functional adults, we are aware that life is not fair, and we accept that and move on. Usually, we don't have a fit of anger that debilitates us or renders us unable to function. I find that many kids on the spectrum act out when they perceive something as unfair.

To help a child see fairness differently, I use this explanation: If there were a food shortage in the world, and authorities were distributing bags of food, would it be fair for them to give every family two bags of food? That might sound fair at first, but if there were five people in my family and only two in yours, would it be fair to give both our families an equal amount? Equal is not fair. I propose to them that everyone getting what they need is fair, which makes the concept of fairness more concrete. This is a great example to use with children who have siblings on the spectrum and have trouble understanding why the rules are different for the brother or sister with autism.

One little boy attended kindergarten in a school where the kids who rode the bus left 15 minutes before the kids who walked home; the "bussers" were allowed to leave at 3:15 and the "walkers" at 3:30. The boy perceived this system to be unfair and asked his teacher why it was that way. When he didn't get an answer that satisfied him, he decided it was unfair and took matters into his own hands. He simply left school early to walk home which, of course, caused a big problem for the teacher on bus duty. These kids can be so rigid that when they perceive that something is not fair, they become angry and may take unusual or dramatic action.

The anger and frustration of individuals on the spectrum can erupt at the slightest provocation, making them appear to display characteristics of bipolar disorder, which encompasses extreme highs followed by extreme lows (see Appendix B.) This behavior does fit the autistic character. The black and white way of thinking brings with it a black and white emotional state. Everything seems to be either all right (a display of true happiness, if very rare) or, at the other end of the continuum, all wrong; emotions run hot or cold. The problem with this, and a key point in treatment, is that these kids can get into intense angry episodes seemingly at the drop of a hat. In many cases, these individuals have spent days, if not weeks, holding in these intense feelings, and then they seem to explode suddenly and without warning.

It is the old "kicking-the-dog" adage. Why do people kick the dog when they come home from work? Is it because of the dog's behavior, or is it because of a bad day at work? Whether it involves an individual with autism or not, negative emotional energy has to, and eventually will, erupt. Everyone has a different breaking point. If we do not find appropriate ways to deal with our anger and frustration, that anger will surface in our behavior. With children on the spectrum who have not developed coping skills, this sudden expression of intense feeling is very common.

A young man on the spectrum described his emotional state to me in the following fashion: When he was frustrated, he felt layers of anger building up inside of him. He tried to suppress this emotional volcano by "pushing" the layers down. The problem, he reported, was that the slightest incident of anger could cause the layers to immediately surface and he would explode. He did not know how to deal with the anger and process it effectively, so he just suppressed it until, finally, something would trigger it and he would lose control of his temper. Needless to say, this tendency has caused him much trouble at school.

One young man articulated to me how he feels when he gets home after a day of overload at school. He described what he calls the "Hulk smash syndrome." When the Hulk loses control of himself in a fit of rage, he changes from a typical guy to a bulky green monster. That's how this boy feels when he returns home from school.

Another adolescent with autism described getting angry in fourth and fifth grade; he would sometimes become aggressive. He said that he was afraid of getting angry. He knew that he might get aggressive and suffer the consequences that may ensue as a result of his actions. He also intentionally tried to avoid any social situations that he perceived might result in his feeling angry. Again, he is suppressing his anger, trying to white-knuckle his way through his feelings.

When I teach parents and their children about autism, I use Diagram 11.1 to describe the eruption of anger that often occurs. It provides a visual that shows the buildup of layers of emotion, which is usually followed by an explosion if that emotion is not addressed or dealt with effectively.

In most cases, neuro-typical individuals learn to contain negative emotions until it is safe to express them with the least possibility of trouble. For these children, this is done in an environment where they feel safe, primarily at home and usually with their mothers (where they feel the safest). Children follow this pattern because, for the most part, even as little ones, they are able to understand the ramifications of angry behavior at school. We all know from an early age that we can express our frustrations at home with far less implications. This may be, in part, because of the clear and unwavering boundaries and consequences in place at school. Often boundaries at home are more relaxed, or less clear.

For individuals with ASD who are unable to control their emotions and lack the social understanding to realize that some environments are safer, the blowups can (and do) happen anywhere, including school. Some of these kids are able to maintain control at school to avoid trouble and to avoid drawing attention to themselves but, often, they

ERUPTION

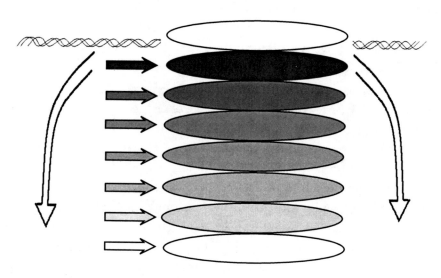

Diagram 11.1 - The shaded arrows on the left of the circles indicate the rising emotional intensity, getting darker as intensity grows. Once the emotional buildup is beyond the spiraled line, which represents the individual's threshold of tolerance, an eruption of emotion occurs. The arrows pointing down the outside indicate the calming and return to a normal emotional state that occurs after the eruption.

still have trouble at home. They may even have a different attitude about what is required of their behavior at home where rules may be less rigidly enforced.

In addition, children without autism are intrinsically socially motivated, and naturally learn to keep things together while in social situations, such as when they are at school with peers, so that they don't get singled out. They learn how to channel their anger appropriately. Many individuals with autism lack this intrinsic motivation. This inability to process their emotions appropriately may result in problems in the school environment, which, in turn, may result in their being singled out. This occurs when life doesn't meet their expectations, when what they want to happen, or expect to happen, does not happen as they think it should. Unable to effectively verbalize what is troubling them, they become noticeably upset, and often resort to very primitive ways to express their anger, even resorting to aggression.

Anger is a very familiar emotion for children on the spectrum; they must live in a world not designed or built for them. Understanding where the child is on an emotional level enables parents and educators to teach strategies that help the child deal with eruptions and help prevent anger from controlling their lives.

CHAPTER 12

SAVANTS

The interesting point about savant skills is that they all relate to concrete, black and white kinds of information—information that doesn't change. Savants demonstrate the ultimate in linear processing.

T he term savant is derived from the French word *savoir*, which means *to know*, and from the Latin word *sapere*, which means *to be wise*. Savant syndrome is a rare condition in which a person affected with a mental disability (such as autism or mental retardation) exhibits exceptional skill or brilliance in some limited field. This brilliance, or talent, is so spectacular because it is contrasted with the person's developmental limitations. The condition may be congenital or it can be acquired later in childhood or even into adulthood.

The skills a savant may exhibit are usually linked with prodigious memory in one of five general areas: music, art, mathematical calculations, calendar calculations, or mechanical/spatial ability. Commonly, savant behaviors include obsessive preoccupation with, and memorization of, music, sports trivia, airline flight schedules, maps, or historical facts. Some savants develop an unbelievable ability to hear a musical piece and play it back from memory after hearing it only once. Research has found that individuals with autism who have savant skills in music can distinguish pitch better than most famous composers; however, they struggle with composing their own music, which is a more abstract ability.

Calendar calculating, common among savants, extends beyond the ability to name the day of the week on which a date will occur in any given year; calendar calculating includes being able to identify which years over the next 100 in which Easter will fall on March 23, for example, or when July 4 will fall on a Tuesday.[1] This is much more than memorization; in fact, a number of recent studies show that savant abilities extend far beyond memorization; rote memory alone cannot account for the presence of many of these extraordinary savant skills.

EXPRESSION OF SAVANT-LIKE SKILLS

The interesting point about savant skills is that they all relate to concrete, black and white kind of information—information that doesn't change. Savants demonstrate the ultimate in linear processing. It is no surprise, then, that up to 60% of all savants are autistic and that savant abilities occur in as many as 10% of autistic persons.[2]

I want to emphasize the distinction between a true savant and someone with savant-like abilities. A true savant is off the charts in one area, like math, yet functions at a low level in all other areas. In the movie *Rain Man*, Dustin Hoffman's character, Raymond Babbitt, an autistic savant, cannot make change for a dollar, but he can instantly compute square roots of large numbers in his head. Raymond is considered a prodigious savant; it is believed that there are fewer than 50 prodigious savants living today. He is the exception, not the rule.

Often, I work with individuals on the spectrum who develop savant-like skills; they are not true savants because they have high levels of skill in many areas, yet there is one area in which they are exceptional.

---

1 http://www.wisconsinmedicalsociety.org/physicians

2 *ibid.*

As a result, that's where they direct their energy and allocate their resources. I think what happens is that they see a calendar one day, the next day they get up, look at it, and it's the same! They think, "Nothing else around me is the same, but this calendar is the same. I'm going to flip back a couple of months. Oh, it's the same every time I look at it! This is fantastic. I'm going to memorize it. I'm going to spend time doing this!" If you ask someone who has memorized years of calendars, "On what day of the week did November 3, 1927 fall?" he will have the answer ready: "Tuesday."

There is a neurological difference between memorizing and calculating. Some individuals may appear to be calculating when they are actually memorizing. For instance, if someone asks you to give the answer to 8 x 8, most people can immediately answer 64. How do we know that answer so quickly? We memorized the multiplication table, and the answer just pops into our heads. Memorization takes concentrated effort, but it is a different neurological process than calculating. If you were asked to add 16 and 34, you probably have not memorized that answer, but I'll bet you could calculate it quickly because you have no doubt had many occasions in which you needed to add two-digit numbers. Adding those two numbers is an example of a neurological algorithm.

An algorithm is a step-by-step procedure used to solve a problem, usually associated with math and computer science. Any time the brain performs a task, it is completing an algorithm. However, by repeating the algorithm multiple times, the brain creates a pathway that it remembers. Consider that professional quarterback who throws the football in a game with no conscious thought about the steps involved. When he first learned to do this task, however, his brain was calculating every step in the task. Practice turned the process into an automatic activity. The more you repeat a task, whatever that task may be, the faster the brain transitions from processing or computing the steps (performing an algorithm) to automatically following the steps (memorizing the pathway).

Savants develop very strong neurological algorithms that allow them to compute tasks quickly in their heads. It's true that there is a high degree of memorization involved, but it is not solely memorization. When they are interested in something, savants apply concentrated, motivated effort to learning about that topic; savants become extreme experts in one area of interest. Research suggests that a person becomes an expert after 10,000 hours of motivated practice, or 10 years of focus in one area. Savants spend all their free time studying their particular interest; they are motivated to study that one specific subject and, as a result, they develop complex neurological algorithms that enable them to answer seemingly difficult questions quickly and accurately.

A key word when explaining these special savant-like abilities is *motivation*. Why are individuals with autism so motivated to focus on one area? This hyperfocus serves a couple of purposes. First, it is used for tuning out the external world, which is either overbearing or makes no sense. In addition, studying something that doesn't change is calming to them; studying static information helps create the sameness that is comfortable. Once they hear a piece of music, it never changes in their heads; the pitch stays the same. The days of the week on a calendar never change, ever. Math facts stay the same.

Individuals on the spectrum can have a focus on almost anything. One child with whom I worked had an obsessional interest in stoplights. He knew how and where they were made, what they cost to make, and how they were transported. He could explain in detail how a stoplight worked. For Halloween, he dressed (you guessed it) as a stoplight. He was in first grade and had considerable social difficulties because of his stoplight obsession. What do you think he always wanted to chat about? Yes, stoplights. Remember that, with these kids, the conversation is not reciprocal; there is no give and take in the dialogue. He would talk about stoplights and he didn't worry about whether or not the other student wanted to learn about their intricacies. He was a stoplight expert; he exhibited savant-like skills in this one area.

As I mentioned earlier, I also had an incredible experience with a little boy who exhibited savant-like skills with maps. Those of you who travel with young children know what it is like to be in the car with kids for a long time. We all know the refrain, "Are we there yet? Are we there yet, Dad?" Before we even get to the interstate! Not this little boy; he knows exactly where his family is going because he has memorized the route. He doesn't need to ask where they are, because he watches the mile markers. So, when his neuro-typical sister starts asking, "Are we there yet?" mom and dad will say to him, "Hey Joe, how much farther?" And, he'll answer, "26 miles." "What exit are we taking?" "32." Imagine how powerful that little boy's mind could be if he could find a way to channel that energy into a productive life skill, which I have no doubt he will.

About five years ago, this same child was in my office and I mentioned that I was going to a family reunion. He asked me where I was going and when I answered, "Benton Beach campground in Minnesota," he began to detail the route, outlining all the roads I should take. "You wanna take 90-94 and when you get to Minneapolis, take 694 over the overpass. Then you take 694 and it turns into 94 again and then you're gonna take highway C north at St. Cloud. You take highway C about 11 miles and then you're gonna take highway D, and then it's about two miles down the road on your right." This was off the top of his head without looking at anything!

As he was talking, I was writing everything down. Then I checked Mapquest, and guess what? He was absolutely right. Had he ever been to Minnesota? No, never. Now, I've gone to this campground for five years, and I still need to check Mapquest before I leave home to figure out the exit that I need to take for the reunion. I should remember these things, but I can't. It's their obsession that becomes important to these kids, not football and not socializing; it's focusing on what they like, and deriving the benefits of dealing with concrete information—calming themselves and tuning out the environment. If their focus does happen to be football, that works to their advantage because they are very popular on Monday (since they know all the stats). The problem for these kids arises when they do not know when to stop talking about football! One of the things you don't see is a social savant. It's too gray, too dynamic. People can be good at being social, but you can't have a savant skill in that area, it doesn't exist.

The girl on TV who won the national spelling bee studies spelling words; she enjoys studying and is motivated by it. However, studying so intensely may compromise her ability to be social and to develop her mirror neurons. She is extremely motivated to study spelling words at the expense of her social life.

When it comes to your child who is on the spectrum, the important thing to realize is that if he is motivated to study a particular area of interest, you can help him use that interest as a way of engaging in social interaction. Teach him to make conversation using this interest. Basically, encourage your child to prepare a few interesting facts about his interest that he might want to share. Then, when he is in a conversation, he may ask if the other person(s) would be interested in hearing about his favorite topic. After mentioning his three facts, the child should learn to ask the listener what she thinks. You want to teach them how to share their interests without boring the other person with too much detail. I describe this more fully in Chapter 15, Treatment and Techniques, under the section called *My Time and Your Time.*

Chapter 13

Foundations for Effective Treatment

Teaching children the skills that help them maneuver in a world that requires social contact is not the same thing as imposing a normal lifestyle.

*T*he main goal I have for my clients who have autism is to make them happy and functional in their lives. They need to learn how to navigate and be effective in a social world. They do not have to like it, they just have to be able to do it. Even the most introverted neuro-typical individuals are still socially functional. They are able to go through a checkout lane at the supermarket or speak to a teller at the bank, accomplishing what they need to accomplish to survive and to create a life that makes them happy, even though they may prefer to be at home. That's what the kids I treat need to learn—to become socially functional. They may never be extroverted social butterflies, but I want them to be functional in a world that requires social contact. Most of all, I want them to be happy.

Know the Goal of Treatment

Kids with ASD need to learn to accept life for what it is—unpredictable, ever-changing and, in many cases, abstract. Again, they don't have to like it, they just have to accept it, and be able to work within its parameters. Living a functional life may not look like what we expect or consider normal, but that doesn't mean it's not successful for the individual. For example, my chemistry and physics teacher in high school, whom I'll call Dr. L., earned Ph.D. degrees for fun. Over summers and holiday breaks, he took classes to earn another advanced degree. I don't even know how to pronounce some of the degrees that he has received, but that's how he filled his spare time.

Dr. L. was not married. He would always come to class wearing the same black shoes, the same style of black pants, and the same white shirt with a colored pin stripe that matched his tie (red stripe with red tie, blue stripe with blue tie, etc.). One day in class, I asked him, "Dr. L., didn't you have the red tie on last Thursday?" He stopped his lecture and said, "Well, yes, Tim, I always wear the red tie on Thursday, and I have ten pairs of black pants that are all from JC Penney and I wear a new one every day, and I have different shirts that are white with stripes and I wear the red stripe on Thursday and the green stripe on Wednesday..." and he continued through the entire week, detailing the color and the day. Then he continued to tell me that at the end of the week he takes all those dirty clothes to the laundromat, and slides the next set (which was, apparently, hanging ready to go in his closet) down into position in his closet where last week's clothes were hanging. Then he returned to his class lecture. You know, I was thinking that I had kind of caught him and I was teasing him a little bit, but when he finished the description of his wardrobe methodology, I sat there with my mouth open, dumbfounded with nothing to say.

Looking back on it from my vantage point now, I am willing to bet that Dr. L. was on the spectrum. He definitely appeared quirky. If he was walking down the hall, and you said hello to him, he'd make a quick hand up waving gesture and keep walking. If there happened to be a fight going on, he'd step over the two kids rolling around on the ground, and just keep going.

Dr. L. was strange, but he loved to teach, and he was probably one of the most amazing teachers I ever had. I still remember some of his lessons. One day, he was talking about gravity, and he shot a BB across the room. It fell in a little coffee can as it dropped. He said, "Doesn't matter the velocity of the BB, as long as it gets over there, it will land in the can every time." I'm thinking "No way!" Plink. Everybody says, "Do it again!" Plink. Plink. Plink. I still remember some of the experiments he showed us; he was truly an amazing teacher. When he stood before the class, he knew exactly what he was going to say. He held his notes in front of him, and he'd answer any question on the subject of physics or chemistry.

He owned this old, beat-up Datsun, and I remember asking him, "Why don't you get a new car?" He looked at me like I was from another planet. "Why would I do that?" he asked me. "Well, your door's gonna fall off. It's all rusted out," I replied. "No, Tim, this works just fine. It gets me from home to where I need to be—here at work."

One day, he told me a story that blew me away. He said he had taken a doctorate class in which his professor had told them, "Nobody will ace this class." Of course, Dr. L. decided that he was going to do just that. He said to me, "Tim, there was one question that everybody else missed on the test. This professor asked what was written on the gravestone of one of the physicists we were studying. I knew the answer." I asked him, "How could you possibly know that?" He replied, "Oh, I had read a book about that physicist."

Well, as a high school student, I was amazed. I asked him, "Did you have to read the book? Why would you read a book that's not assigned?" He answered, "No, I didn't have to read it, I just read it to study." Which prompted me to ask him, "How would you possibly have time to do that?" And he replied, "Well, I study 22 hours a day, and I sleep for two." Learning is what motivated him.

The reason I tell that story is that we have to be very careful about what type of lifestyle we try to impose, or want to impose on these individuals. When kids on the spectrum come to my office, I do not try to choose a lifestyle for them; I just want them to be happy and functional. Dr. L. was happy and functional. He never married, drove a wreck of a car, fixed TVs and VCRs for fun, and studied 22 hours a day, but he had figured out how to manage life's necessities; he learned to live within the structure of the social world, hold a job, and support his lifestyle. He was one of the best teachers I ever had, and he loved what he did; it made him happy. From his point of view, his life was successful.

So, when we're working with kids with ASD, we have to be careful about imposing what we consider to be our social values. Teaching children the skills that help them maneuver in a world that requires social contact is not the same thing as imposing a normal lifestyle. I just want them to be functional. I want to make sure they can go online or to the bank. I want to make sure they can manage daily tasks. I want to make sure that they don't turn people in to the authorities because their time cards are two minutes over. That's what I mean by functional—able to get along in the world. I teach them functional skills so that they can choose their own lifestyle, rather than letting the difficulties that arise from their autism control the choices that are available to them.

EFFECTIVELY COMMUNICATING WITH CHILDREN
ON THE SPECTRUM

To effectively communicate with kids who have ASD, I offer some simple, easy-to-follow principles that help facilitate understanding and reduce frustration. When speaking with children on the spectrum, use objective information, (i.e., concrete, factual information) rather than subjective information. If the child is agitated or upset, she may prefer to be alone. This is not a reflection on you, she may just need time and

rocess. If you are with a child who is upset, talk less and ask
.uestions. Even speak in a softer tone. Give her a chance to
.s.

The recipe for talking to kids and eliciting the best results includes using positive reinforcement, focusing on what they are doing correctly, and rewarding appropriate behavior. It's important to let them set the pace, respecting their need for processing time. In a school setting, consider rewarding the entire class for good behavior so the child with autism does not feel different or singled out.

Keep in mind this very simple concept as you are planning and working out strategies for individuals on the spectrum. All behavior has a purpose, unless the individual is psychotic. The challenge is to figure out what purpose is behind the behavior. There usually is an antecedent to the behavior, so looking for the ABC pattern I described in Chapter 8, Understanding Characteristics of ASD, is very effective. Remember, these kids are just like you and me, but their experience is times 10!

Making Accommodations vs. Fitting in "As Is"

I agree with those who feel that it is important to teach the neurotypical world about working with individuals who are on the spectrum, and to ask them to adjust things to accommodate the difficulties of those on the spectrum. I do this whenever I can. The problem is that, in this day and age, many people and institutions do not or cannot make accommodations.

Today, in 2010, when I am trying to help individuals on the spectrum find work, the world's financial strain does not make it an easy task. In light of the problems in the economy, it is very challenging to ask managers to make accommodations when so many people are vying for every job. I am not saying that they shouldn't make the accommodations, I encourage them to do so, but it can be difficult when jobs are in demand and there are 10 other candidates who don't need any special accommodations.

We can't depend on the world's accommo
the problem of fitting in. Teaching those with
the constraints of a normal environment wit'
tions is a more successful strategy to help then
I teach individuals on the spectrum that they
they fit in. This helps them learn that the one tʜᴉⁿ◡
they do have control over is themselves, not others!

ADDRESS BEHAVIORAL ISSUES IN THERAPY

When I consult with a family for the first time, our initial focus is
typically on any behavioral difficulties (which are probably what
caused them to seek treatment). Those are the first things that need to
be explored and understood. Once we have addressed (or begun to
address) behavioral issues, we can shift our focus to the other challenges
that the child faces, and begin to teach the parents how to work with
the autism. Understanding the need to use linear language, create a
more linear environment, and provide motivation are important shifts
to make.

EDUCATE FAMILIES ABOUT UNDERSTANDING AUTISM

To reiterate, autistic information processing is not wrong, it is just
different. Understanding and taking that difference into account is the
first step in developing treatment. My goal is to teach parents and
educators to understand how children on the spectrum think; once they
understand this, the adults are better able to communicate with these
children in a way that makes sense to them—to speak their language,
and thus be more able to effect change in their lives. The ability to
communicate is a prerequisite for creating an effective treatment solu-
tion, and it also helps you to maintain your patience when you understand that this is a true exceptionality and not just a case of stubborn
refusal to be cooperative. Distinguishing that difference is tough.

en, I find myself saying to frustrated and confused parents, "...s the autism." This is especially true in higher functioning individuals whose autistic issues can be interpreted in another way rather than attributed to ASD. It's easy to believe that the child is just uncooperative for refusing to do something that is asked of him, just because you said so. The truth is that they often do not understand why they should do it, they don't see what's in it for them, and they need that motivation to inspire them to confront and overcome the difficulty they face to accomplish what is being asked of them. Think about it. We all know exercise is healthy and beneficial for us. So, why are so many people out of shape? Because exercise is difficult and sometimes painful. Imagine if every minor task required that level of motivation to accomplish!

Understanding the challenges that children with autism face is essential to understanding them. It's easy to write off a kid as simply being mean or rude when they blurt out a comment that seems inappropriate or unkind. Sometimes saying what is on their minds is misinterpreted as being mean or trying to start a fight when they do not understand what is wrong with what they said. As I have already discussed, individuals with autism sometimes struggle with the white lie, or with small talk. Not because they do not want to engage in social chatter, but because it is hard for them, given their neurological architecture.

One of the most dynamic differences between neuro-typical individuals and those on the spectrum is that people with ASD think in a very concrete, linear way, while those of us without ASD can understand abstractions. Knowing this difference is crucial to communicating with them effectively. Those on the spectrum respond better to linear language, i.e., straight forward language with no ambiguity or shades of gray. For example, "I will be back in 10 minutes" is preferable to "I will be back in a little while." From this vantage point, the difficulty interacting with these individuals becomes clear. They often do not understand our language and, therefore, get easily frustrated and angry when we try to communicate. Adjusting your communication to be linear and concrete is a giant leap toward working effectively with your child. This linear approach is a skill that can be taught to families.

Providing the motivation the child needs is important, too. For example, when parents do not clearly delineate what they are asking the child to do and what benefit is in it for the child, the child does not understand the why behind what he is being asked to do. In other words, saying, "Take out the garbage" may not make sense to a child on the spectrum. He might reason that it is not his house, he did not create the garbage, and he doesn't care if the garbage stays in the house or gets put out in the trash can. These children cannot piece together other information, even though it may seem obvious or logical to the rest of us. For example, the fact that everyone in the house does chores, or that chores need to be done regularly, will not even be considerations. However, if a parent says, "First you have to take out the garbage and then you can play your video game," it makes more sense to the child. The message is more linear. The child knows what is in it for him if he takes out the garbage.

When we not only communicate in the linear language they understand, but also create a more linear environment surrounding them, they do much better, they are not as frustrated, and their anxiety levels decrease. Ultimately, we do need to teach children on the spectrum to see and understand the shades of gray that exist in life. This takes time and patience, and is only accomplished by having a solid frame of reference and framework of experience in the child's life to build upon. Establishing a more structured, linear environment and improving communication are two huge first steps which reduce stress and provide an environment conducive to intervention and treatment.

CORE COMPONENTS FOR TREATMENT

There are two core components for a good treatment plan:

- We need to tap into the strengths of individuals on the spectrum, and focus on what they do well, taking that information and teaching them how to use those strengths to help them succeed in areas that are challenging.

- We need to empower individuals with ASD to be proactive and take control over the areas in their lives that they feel are out of their control, like social interactions.

Applying the first of these concepts involves taking skills they have, such as being able to focus on details, and teaching them how to use the same strategies that make them successful at that to become more functional socially. For example, I will ask the verbal individuals who want to talk about their topic of interest incessantly, to employ a very linear strategy when interacting with a peer. I tell them to offer three ideas about their favorite topic, and then ask the person to whom they are talking if he would like to hear more. Children with ASD need to be taught to use this strategy; they also need to learn how to handle themselves if the other person says that he does not want to hear more. Techniques like this tap into the individual's strengths to help make social interactions more manageable and successful.

The second concept is that those on the spectrum need to be taught that using their strengths to be more proactive, rather than reactive, will make them feel better about themselves and can reduce stress in general. Being proactive and taking control can be tricky for these kids. In addition to teaching them to take control over themselves and their minds, they also need to understand that they can't control everything. Their sphere of influence has limits; the only thing an individual truly has control over is himself. A child on the spectrum often tries to control whatever he can within his immediate environment to reduce stress, including things like the way he keeps his bedroom or the placement of furniture in the house.

It is important to their success in life that individuals with autism understand how to be proactive about their lives and their own needs and balance that with the appropriate kind of control. As they get older and life's demands become greater, this inability to control can create anxiety, stress, and a great deal of anger.

Teaching children to control their feelings regardless of what others are doing or saying to them is a necessary life skill. I challenge individuals on the spectrum not to let others control them. I frequently tell them that other people cannot control their feelings, only they can control them. I try to teach them that things may change in their environment, but they (and no one else) decide if they are going to let it bother them. This is part of teaching them how to control themselves and their emotional reaction(s).

Let me make a critical distinction. I rarely try to change their perspective or their beliefs (e.g., not liking homework or school); rather, I try to teach them to control their emotions so they are able to effectively do their homework and learn to tolerate school, even though they still don't like it. Remember, it's all about functionality, not about specific opinions.

Teaching these kids that they can't control everything and that they need to do what they don't want to do just because it is the right thing to do is a pivotal step in treatment. Once they have learned to do what they don't want to do, and have become more proactive, we can teach them other effective compensation strategies, for example, using visual systems such as notes, schedules, and pictures.

CHAPTER 14

CREATING EFFECTIVE STRATEGIES/INTERVENTIONS

All children need structure and consistency; they need rules to live by, yet they resist them. Children on the spectrum need control and consistency, times 10, and they will resist them, times 10.

*P*rogramming and interventions force change for individuals with autism; we force them out of their linear world and into our social world every time we intervene in their natural pattern of existing. Strategies that I have found to be most effective for individuals with autism have a few underlying consistencies. These strategies:

- Address sensory issues
- Are framed in black and white
- Are quantitative not qualitative
- Use the individual's inherent gifts
- Teach discipline (learn to do what they don't want to do just because)
- Teach the benefits of social interaction
- Have continuity across environments
- Focus on rewards rather than punishment

Let's look at each of these factors individually. First, we need to make sure that we evaluate the sensory needs of individuals on the spectrum. They may need to have a sensory diet in place (a specific limit to, or combination of sensory input) that helps them regulate (i.e., maintain homeostasis) so they can engage in different activities and interventions. They may need the lights turned down, or they may need breaks built into the day that allow their systems to calm down and regulate. Most children on the spectrum need to be taught how to recognize when their systems are in need of a break, how to ask for a break appropriately, and what to do that will help them calm themselves. Sensory regulation must be achieved before any other strategy can have a full effect.

Second, for a strategy to make sense to them, and therefore be effective in teaching them how to function in a social world, that strategy must be black and white, i.e., relate to their black and white approach to processing the world. For example, a visual schedule is a concrete, black and white outline of what is going to happen during their day. This reduces their anxiety by removing the unknowns from their day.

This leads us directly to the third strategy. Information presented to them should be quantitative rather than qualitative. Visual systems that use numbers and lists are concrete ways to relate information that is abstract so that it makes sense to an individual with autism. Remember the boy who watched the mile markers on a long drive? That was his way of making the trip quantitative (marked in tangible miles, rather than in the qualitative, "we're almost there" abstract), which made it more manageable for him.

Fourth, we want to teach these individuals to take advantage of their inherent gifts, while at the same time enhancing their social abilities. For most, their gifts include the ability to focus on details and to control. I teach individuals on the spectrum to focus on controlling their actions, paying attention in school, and paying attention to what they say in a social interaction. This also applies to paying attention and listening to the teacher. They can even plan out what to say or what they want to talk about prior to a social interaction. They can study current events or the most current sports scores and use that information in conversations. In this way, they put their natural gifts to work by bringing the concrete details that make sense to them into their daily life and interactions.

Fifth, we need to teach them that sometimes they have to do things that they do not want to do. This is a big one; they have to do many things that they would not choose to do, if given their own way. They do not want to do chores, go to school, do homework, do what other people say, play someone else's game, etc., but they have to learn to do these things in order to be functional. What prevents them from being functional is when they get stuck and are unable to do what they do not want to do. For example, some kids don't want to do homework, so they take all night to get it done (or they take all night and won't get it done) because they cannot get themselves to do it. For apparent survival reasons, they have to be able to do things they don't want to do to get by in the world. Without that skill, they will struggle to be functional adults.

Sixth, attempt to teach individuals on the spectrum the benefits of social interactions as they pertain to them. They need to internalize the concept that getting their thoughts and needs acknowledged is valuable, important, and rewarding. They need to learn that it can be fun to share stories or to play games with other people; it is fun to laugh and tell jokes. It is fun to play Pictionary in my office and compete with another team. When the individuals I treat come to my groups, they get to experience what it is like to sit with their peers, to get a turn to talk, and to keep up with what is being discussed. They begin to enjoy social interaction. They want to come to group to hang out with their peers. They get to experience first hand the pleasure and satisfaction of successful interpersonal communication.

Next, it is important to have continuity across all environments; deliver one constant message on every channel. That means that educators, family members, and therapists need to have a united front and work together to agree on requirements, approaches, and consequences. This not only prevents the child from slipping between the cracks, as we discussed in the case of the boy who told his teachers that his work was at home and told his parents that his work was at school, but it reduces confusion and builds clarity.

Finally, I advocate strategies that earn rewards rather than lose privileges as this provides motivation rather than punishment. Creating effective treatment, these elements work together to move an individual on the spectrum from their rigid, black and white world closer to the unpredictable, social, abstract world that they must fit into in order to prosper in life.

IMMEDIATE GRATIFICATION

Immediate gratification is important with children on the spectrum because they have trouble seeing long-term rewards or working toward long-term goals. They tend to do better when their reward is given shortly after the desired behavior has occurred. "Good behavior equals a reward" is a more concrete concept that is easier for them to understand. For example, "Take out the garbage, earn some video time." When the reward immediately follows the task or chore, it helps the child on the spectrum connect the reward to the behavior, thus they know what is in it for them.

Reducing any gap in time between the behavior and the reward also reduces the chance that a child will "throw in the towel," so to speak, believing that he has ruined his chance for a reward on the upcoming weekend with bad behavior on Monday. If a child gives up on the possibility of the reward, there would be no motivation for him to work hard during the week.

STARTING WITH THE BASICS (CHAINING OF INFORMATION/TEACHING PREREQUISITES)

During my early research, I interviewed a man with autism who described his frequent frustrations. For example, when he was taught to eat as a child, he said that all the utensils were placed in front of him and he was instructed on what utensil to use for what portion of the meal, however, he was not taught how to hold the utensils. He was frustrated because he felt he did not know how to hold them properly. Teaching prerequisites and basics may be a pivotal factor in the effectiveness of an intervention. We cannot assume that individuals on the spectrum know the prerequisites of what we are trying to teach. It is best to assume that they do not know the basics until they can prove that they do. So, when teaching any skill, build up from the basics.

FOLLOW THROUGH IS CRUCIAL AND TOUGH

All children, on the autistic spectrum or not, need structure and consistency; they need rules to live by, yet they resist them. Children on the spectrum need control and consistency, times 10, and they will resist it, times 10. That makes consistent follow through all the more imperative, and all the more tough! The challenge that parents, teachers, or therapists face, is that what might take five or 10 exposures to teach a new idea or to make a point to an individual not on the spectrum, may take 10 times as long for someone on the spectrum to learn. If you do the math, that's potentially 50 to 100 exposures!

Whenever parents or teachers implement any strategies, they need to follow through, establishing long-term consistency whenever possible. Consistent follow through is crucial for intervention to be effective. Kids on the spectrum are very rule-oriented, routine-driven individuals. Therefore, once new routines are established, they will be most comfortable with the least amount of additional change. Another motivator for parents is that any slip on their part may reset the learning curve back to the beginning.

Children with ASD are incredibly persistent; they can hyperfocus on a topic or on what they want. These kids are more persistent than those of us who don't have a child on the spectrum can begin to fathom. Each time they ask for something, and you say "no," a second later it is a new time, so they ask again, testing to see if the boundary is still intact.

Recently, my middle daughter wanted a guinea pig. She was incredibly persistent—asking, and asking, and asking about it. Even after I said, "No, absolutely not," she would talk about it from time to time. Maybe she would bring it up a few times a day…then, just when I would think that she had finally given up, she'd ask again. It was a real parenting effort to effectively handle her insistent desire for this pet. I have sympathy for the parents whose children on the spectrum get stuck on a topic or something that they want, and they ask 10 times as much as my daughter asked for that guinea pig! Exhausting!

Getting people with ASD to adopt a new habit, behavior, or pattern that does not come naturally to them will require time for them to stretch their thinking and adapt to the change. That means that our effectiveness in guiding these children toward more functional, healthier ways of living for the long-term is directly impacted by our ability to remain steadfast even after we have experienced some positive results. It is human nature to become complacent; we have to try to avoid complacency and reverting to old habits. Consistency takes focus, effort, and determination. Our determination to see positive change needs to be greater than the child's drive and determination to maintain consistency. When you think about it that way, it's a daunting task!

Parents and teachers are only human, and, unfortunately, once something works, what is our natural tendency as human beings? To get away from the very thing that made it work. For example, think about losing weight. For most people, dieting is the simplest thing conceptually to figure out how to accomplish. You change your lifestyle; you eat fewer calories than you burn each day. A colleague once said to me, "If knowledge equaled behavior, everybody would be at their ideal weight." You lose weight, you're feeling good, and then you start creeping back to eating some of the things you shouldn't be eating. Maybe you get too busy, so you stop working out as often, and you undo the good you did. When we start interventions, we need to stick to them, and avoid becoming complacent. We have to be disciplined and stick to what works!

CHAPTER 15

TREATMENTS AND TECHNIQUES

There is a direct correlation between someone's cognitive experience and his behavior. Anytime we impact the thinking of an individual, we impact his behavior.

T his chapter explores some basic techniques and treatment strategies that can help parents and teachers work effectively with children on the spectrum.

These techniques can help you: 1) better communicate with individuals on the spectrum; 2) create an environment that is better suited for an individual with ASD; 3) learn how to intervene at important points to change behavior; and 4) learn how to teach individuals on the spectrum to control their emotions.

There is a direct correlation between someone's cognitive experience and his behavior. Anytime we impact the thinking of an individual, we impact his behavior. When intervention causes a decrease in linear thinking and an increase in social processing, thinking changes, and thus behavior also begins to change. This connection between experience and behavior is implied as one of the fundamental principals of the control theory.

The shift from a linear world to a social world that is spurred on by treatment forces a reallocation of the focus, resources, energy, and motivation in individuals on the spectrum. They begin to develop in a more social context and, as a result, they take in more of the external environment. By managing their behavior and their thinking, we are attempting to change brain neurology and the level of brain functioning in those on the spectrum, creating more interconnectivity and the related flexibility. Individuals with autism would not necessarily choose this route on their own, so extrinsic motivation is often needed to get them to accept change and to be more social.

In the following sections, I provide some techniques and suggestions on methods to affect behavior by creating positive intervention.

VISUALIZATION

A young man named Ryan once told me that he has two sides to his brain, a good side and a bad side. He explained that there was a wall between the good and the bad sides, and when he gets upset, his brain takes a sword and jams it into the wall, puts a hole in it, and then sucks the good into the bad side. This is how he describes what is going on in his life emotionally; he uses a concrete visual image. Eventually, in therapy, we created a mental shield that stops the sword as it tries to come through the wall. Something as simple as that visualization helped him control his mind.

Another one of my clients is a big *Harry Potter* fan; when he gets upset over something, he visualizes himself casting spells that empower him to overcome his problem. You can use visualization techniques to teach a child to learn how to calm himself, such as visualizing a favorite place or activity. I often tell clients, who might be prone to nightmares or other sleeping issues, to imagine one side of the pillow as a good side, and the other as a bad side; then when they are having trouble sleeping, they can just turn the pillow over to the good side.

Visualization is an effective method for changing cognitive experience. Once individuals with autism learn that they can control their brains, therapy can be effective in stimulating other areas of change.

SENSORY BREAKS

A sensory break is an opportunity for a child to do some sort of activity that stimulates them and allows them to neurologically bridge the gap between a heightened sense of stimulation and the point at which they return to homeostasis (refer to Chapter 4, How Autism Develops). In most cases, this means adding stimulus, but in some cases, the child may need a break from any stimulus.

Sensory breaks can be extremely important, especially for the little ones. Children on the spectrum do say that, as they get older, the sensory issues start to diminish, and do not affect them as much. However, even though sensory channel hypersensitivities tend to diminish as children age, the feeling of being overwhelmed in a social situation may not. Children are not going to do well in any setting or environment when they are very young, unless their system is regulated. That is to say, if they are consumed with dealing with the lower level physical/sensory input, they cannot focus on the more challenging aspects of life. Even if your child is not very young, consider addressing sensory overload as a possibility to help gain some control of a difficult situation.

Occupational therapists can often help parents figure out what they need to do to help their children learn to regulate the environment, whether at home or at school. You will get so much more out of these kids if you can get them to regulate, to get the neurons firing appropriately. To do that, you can provide them with the opportunity to take sensory breaks.

For sensory breaks to be effective, we first need to teach these children to recognize when they need a break, and then how to request the break. Requesting a break may not be possible for lower functioning children, so we may need to schedule breaks. I have worked with a number of early childhood teachers and I encourage them to be consistent in allowing for breaks or movement within the classroom. This helps to regulate. Since these children (for the most part) do not recognize that they need a break, we have to provide it for them. Often, these kids don't know how to ask for what they need, especially if they are younger, so creating a simple and clear way to communicate their need for a break can be the first step in getting a child to manage himself, and can prevent a lot of difficulty.

One method is to use a break card. A break card is a communication tool between teacher and student that the student can use any time to indicate his need to engage in any activities that will promote calming himself down. A child is simply given a card that he can show the teacher as a signal that a break is needed.

One of my favorite sensory break activities is having the child do jobs around the school. Have you ever seen a janitor taking the scuff marks off the floor? He attaches a tennis ball to the bottom of a broomstick and rubs the ball back and forth across the mark. Think about the proprioceptive (the body's sense of where one's limbs are in space) feedback a child on the spectrum will receive by engaging in such an activity. They really seem to like this task; it creates an excellent sensory break. I suggest to teachers that they assign the child a certain section of the floor to clean. That's a lot of proprioceptive information.

Asking a child to deliver mail from the classroom to the office is another one of my favorite jobs for a sensory break. If there's no mail, get inventive! Take a manila envelope and put a dictionary in it. The student takes it down to the office…and do you know what the office will have to send back? Another dictionary. In some cases, all that matters is that the task gives the child a break from the stimulation. No one else in the class really knows (or needs to know) that the task is contrived strictly to create a break.

I try to make sure that the sensory breaks make the child appear as normal as possible. This serves two purposes: it helps the child to fit in to the social environment today, and it helps to train the child to select appropriate ways of calming himself in the future (for instance, when he has a job).

Quiet spots are another sensory break option. There should be a specified quiet spot in the classroom that the child can request to retreat to when she needs a break. Sometimes a child just needs time to process what is going on around her and to be removed from all the sensory stimulation in her receptive field.

Another strategy is to use color schemes like stop lights (green, yellow, and red.) Sometimes, if a child doesn't want to call attention to herself, she can hold a certain color pen up in the air. Green might mean "Things are going pretty well." Yellow means "I'm struggling a little bit." Red means "Something needs to happen quickly." Just getting children on the spectrum to recognize that they are nearing a melting point is a step in the right direction (refer to Chapter 16, Strategies for Emotional Regulation, for a more detailed explanation). A child's ability to recognize when she needs to slow down or when she needs a break reduces the behavior issues in the classroom, and, as a bonus, she doesn't alienate herself as much with her classmates.

Ironically, teachers sometimes complain about losing part of their teaching day to sensory breaks. This is a misunderstanding of what a sensory break can mean to a child on the spectrum. Isn't it better to lose 10 minutes to a sensory break than to lose an entire day or class period to a child's being overwhelmed, being disruptive, or having a meltdown? If a child is experiencing sensory overload, what is he getting from the class? Nothing. If he loses a few minutes to gain more productive class time, then I see that as benefit. These children would learn nothing from the class time without the break.

SENSORY BREAKS FOR OLDER KIDS

One day, I was talking to a young man in my office about sensory breaks. He was a regular student in high school; he took classes all day and then spent three hours in football practice after school. (He never really got to play, but he loved the practices.) Then, at home, he got on his mini trampoline and jumped, every single night. I asked him how long he jumped (thinking that his day was already very full). He answered that he jumped for 2½ hours! I could not believe this. I said, "You must take breaks." He replied, "No, but sometimes I go fast, and sometimes I go slowly." I asked him what he was thinking about during that time and he said he was "processing his day."

For those of you who have been on a treadmill, you may appreciate this story. I have an elliptical machine in my basement. My first time on this machine, I set the timer for 20 minutes and started running. There was nothing to look at, no stimulation other than the running. After a little while, I felt like I was nearly done; I looked down at the timer and was shocked to learn that I was only about three minutes into it! I thought there was no way I could do this for 20 minutes. I will go crazy; not due to exhaustion, but to boredom. This young man was on the mini trampoline for 2½ hours, every day, and it was relaxing for him, even meditative. I asked him how long he jumped on days that he did not have school and he said 2½ hours twice a day (that's 5 hours a day)!

It has been reported in the media that one of the most successful men of our time, Bill Gates, has a room in his house that has a trampoline floor. He comes home from work and jumps on the trampoline, which I have heard helps him to process his day; it could be that this computer genius, whose quirkiness fits the profile of someone who falls on the autism spectrum, uses the trampoline to help him calm himself when he is overstimulated. It seems to be working for him—he's doing all right in life. A key to success for individuals on the spectrum is figuring out how to process the sensory world. Once they do this, there is a better chance that they can learn to relax and adapt, allowing their natural talents to surface.

SENSORY BACKPACKS

Another proactive strategy for parents is the sensory backpack. Easily portable, a sensory backpack can be filled with items that allow children to take a break and regulate themselves when they need to. Items such as a coloring book, favorite stuffed animal, video game, or iPod can be kept handy in a backpack for those situations when they are needed.

Having the necessary sensory relief for the child with autism can make life more manageable for the rest of the family. One mother reported an issue with her 12-year-old son with ASD at his brother's fourth grade Christmas concert last year. Because he did not have his sensory backpack and was unable tolerate the lights, sights, and sounds of a crowded auditorium, mom had to leave early and missed her younger son's performance. The next week, she came to therapy frustrated and disappointed in her son with Asperger's disorder. We discussed the use and benefits of a sensory backpack. Guess what happened this year? She and her son with Asperger's were prepared. As a result, the fifth grade Christmas concert went very well, and mom got to see her son perform.

Sensory breaks and sensory backpacks are effective, but we work toward the time when kids, as they grow and develop, can regulate themselves cognitively, rather than with physical stimulus. For example, using self-talk and/or visual processing to control their emotions, thereby, being able to calm themselves with their own words and thoughts and not having to use something physical.

LEAD TIME

Even many neuro-typical individuals do not like abrupt changes in their routines or schedules. When they have time to think and plan for a change, it is much easier to manage. Individuals with ASD are the same way, but to a greater extent (times 10). So another important day-to-day strategy for working effectively with individuals with autism involves providing them with notice in advance of upcoming activities or changes in routine.

This advance warning, or lead time, allows the individual time to process the information at her own pace and to prepare for what is coming up. Telling an individual on the spectrum on Wednesday that he will be going to Grandma's house on Saturday is an example of lead time. The child has time to process the fact that his routine on Saturday is going to change. Even if he likes going to Grandma's house, it is a change, and therefore he has to adapt.

While it may take an extreme change (such as moving or losing a job) to create anxiety in neuro-typical individuals, for individuals with ASD, even a slight change may create that same heightened anxiety. Something as simple as moving the furniture in the living room can do it. Remember the young man who started therapy because his parents moved the couch to make room for the Christmas tree? Again, individuals with ASD want to control their surroundings, and thereby reduce anxiety and unrest in their system. Change creates something unexpected or out of the ordinary.

A word of caution regarding lead time. It is not always helpful to provide too much lead time if the child does not like the activity that is planned. Sometimes, for activities that create a great deal of stress (for example, a visit to the dentist), lead time only serves to create more anxiety, and can cause added stress or sleepless nights until the day actually arrives. In such cases, less lead time can reduce stress for all concerned—the child and, especially, mom and dad. One sleepless night is much easier to manage than two weeks of sleepless nights. So, lead time needs to be balanced with practical considerations.

FIRST/THEN TECHNIQUE

Boundaries work best when the child knows clearly what is expected and what the payoff is, what is in it for them if they comply. This is what the first/then methodology creates. For example, *first* you take out the garbage and *then* you can do what you want. First you do your homework and then you can play on the computer. First you call your grandmother and then you can have your favorite snack.

Even though boundaries exist everywhere, there are no specific instructions as to how to deal with them. This is not spelled out and not intuitive if you are on the spectrum. Both the rules and the exceptions need to be clear. So, you can also say, "Here are the expectations (boundaries) you need to follow in order to get what you want." For example, you explain to your child, "You need to read for thirty minutes every night. If you do, then you can use your cell phone on the weekends. If you do not follow these expectations you will lose the privilege to use the cell phone entirely." This not only creates a clear boundary, but it also allows the child to make a decision about the choices he makes, and the outcome of his choices. Given these boundaries, the child can choose either a good outcome or a bad outcome because both outcomes have been spelled out. This sidesteps the potential loophole in the executive functioning that does not allow him to project the outcome for himself.

ADJUST BOUNDARIES WHEN NECESSARY

Sometimes the rules and boundaries need to be modified to make them more adaptable for the ASD individual. The best teachers that I work with are very structured and consistent while at the same time less rigid than the ASD individual. Let's say that the teacher has a behavior system that takes away tokens that are earned throughout the day. A child who starts with 10 tokens can lose a token for some negative behavior. If the child on the spectrum can either not understand the loss of something that was hers, or cannot handle losing something without a meltdown, the teacher may need to modify the plan to have the child earning tokens but never losing them. This is exactly why I advocate earning privileges rather than losing them. The child may be able to accept, or deal with, not earning a token at some point in her day because she did not follow the rules, but that is very different than taking away something that was already hers—an action that might elicit a very negative, if not dramatic, response.

Another example of modifying boundaries may be to tell a child on the spectrum that he can complete a portion of his chores and then take a break before completing the balance of his chores, versus insisting that he needs to do all of his chores before he can do what he wants (setting the boundary). Maybe this child can only handle two chores and then he legitimately needs a break before completing the other two chores, whereas his siblings can be held accountable for all four chores before they receive any reward. As a parent or teacher trying to motivate a child to learn or follow rules, you may have to adjust the boundary because of what or how much these individuals can handle.

Another example of modifying a boundary would be if a parent's expectation is that the child will spend the entire afternoon with the family on Thanksgiving, but the child can only handle short stints with the family. Mom and dad may need to adjust their expectations in order for their child to be successful that afternoon. The exception that they need to make for their ASD child will most likely be different than for their other children, if they have other children. The other children may experience no distress from being with the family for the entire afternoon without a break. When modifying boundaries to help your child achieve success, it is important for everyone (parents, siblings, educators, fellow students, etc.) to be flexible and adaptable.

MAKE CHOICES MORE CONCRETE

Decision-making can be difficult, if not impossible, for those on the spectrum. They can be "frozen" at times, and can have difficulty seeing the pros and the cons of a situation. Creating a list of the pros and cons can help someone with ASD take a concept that is abstract and make it more concrete in order to process it. For example, someone on the spectrum who is trying to decide if she should apply for a job she saw online can make a list of pros and cons and then evaluate the fact that six pros are more than two cons, therefore she should send in an application for that job.

Whenever the decision-making process can be made more concrete, the likelihood that the individual with ASD will make an appropriate and informed choice increases.

CHECK IN TO DETERMINE "WHERE DID I LOSE YOU?"

Sometimes you can be moving through a conversation and suddenly realize that the individual with ASD has not processed the conversation to the point that would be expected normally. She got lost or got stuck earlier in the conversation. Here's an example of what that looks like. As a graduate student, I was doing therapy with a man with autism. We were sitting in a room with an observation window (like the ones in interrogation rooms), through which my professors and peers could observe us. One day, the professor asked if the man understood what I was explaining to him. I told my professor that I had asked him numerous times if he understood, and he had always replied, "Yes."

Finally, my professor told me that the next time he responds, "Yes," to ask him to explain it back to me. So, the following day, I was doing therapy and my peers were watching me through the one-way glass. I asked the man, "Do you understand?" and I got the expected "Yes" answer. I followed up with, "Can you explain it to me?" He responded, "Nope." I remember feeling everyone looking at me through the glass, and thinking, "How could I have been wrong all this time!" I was embarrassed by my mistaken perception that he had understood what I was saying.

At the time, I didn't understand why he would say he understood me when he clearly didn't. He probably said that to shut me up or to get me to move on, either of which would have cut down on the social interaction, putting an end to his discomfort. This type of behavior is very common.

The image of a tree is a good visual to use to describe how we follow along in a conversation, and what happens when we lose someone in a conversation. Imagine starting the conversation with a broad statement—that is like the trunk of the tree. As the conversation continues, the conversation gets more specific, which is like traveling along one of the limbs of the tree. Then, the conversation progresses to the branches and eventually ends up at the leaves, which represent the most specific information. When an individual on the spectrum gets sidetracked during the conversation, he ends up on a totally different limb, branch, or leaf.

Sometimes, an individual on the spectrum can get caught on a word or phrase that is used during a conversation and get stuck on that word even though the conversation continues. I remember losing a man in conversation and, once I realized this, I asked at what point I had lost him. He replied that when I mentioned the word hammer, it made him think of the hammer he had received for Christmas when he was 5 years old. He went on to say that the recollection of his first hammer led him to recall building a birdhouse with that hammer. This is a completely different train of thought than the discussion I was having with him. He had detoured to a totally different location on the tree.

The way to effectively work with someone on the spectrum is to stop and ask him to explain what was just said to him. In essence, to determine, "Where did I lose you?" By identifying where the individual is stuck, it makes it possible to help him piece together the information you are delivering so that he can understand. This may require listing the logical steps in a progression, providing other data as evidence, slowing down, or presenting the information in another way.

TEACH THEM TO DO IT "JUST BECAUSE"

I have already emphasized the importance of learning to do things just because. This is an especially difficult concept for spectrum individuals since they want to know the why for everything. Often, the reasons that intrinsically motivated people do things will not be the same reasons that make sense to kids who are extrinsically motivated. The best example of extrinsic motivation in our world today is money, but some things in life must be done without getting paid—like brushing your teeth or taking a shower.

When we talk to these kids and tell them, "Well, you know you might get an F in your English class," their response is, "Okay. I don't care. I don't really like English." A grade, in most cases, is not motivating for them at all—they are not intrinsically motivated.

With kids on the spectrum, we need to become more businesslike, providing concrete and specific motivators, such as computer time, alone time, their favorite meal, etc. Even five minutes of free-choice time can be used as an effective motivator. This concrete reward transforms something that they do not want to do into a choice that makes sense to them. Remember the little boy and the social studies questions? The other 24 students in his class answered those questions just because they were asked to do so, but he needed something else.

It isn't wrong that these kids require a different type of motivation. (It is a lot more work for a parent or teacher.) Often, we struggle to understand this aspect of their personality because we assume something should be intrinsically motivating when it is not. So, if you find yourself wondering why a child won't do something that obviously needs to be done, ask yourself if they have any extrinsic motivation. To a child on the spectrum, doing something just because is like working for free. Does anyone want to work for free? Probably not. Extrinsic motivation isn't bad, it's just different. Understanding that and teaching a child to work around their need for a concrete reward is important to long-term functionality. Learning to do something just because is a very important life skill.

PRESENT INFORMATION IN A LINEAR FASHION

A similar technique that I use is piecing information together. Children on the spectrum always ask why, as in, "Why do I have to do this?" When they ask this question, it may be because they cannot see the connection between something they are being asked to do and an outcome that benefits them. For example, if a child who doesn't want to write his English paper asks, "Why should I?" I'll ask him, "Well, what do you want to do for a living?" He may reply that he wants to test video games for a profession. So, I'll ask him, "What do you need to do to get there?" He might reply, "I have to go to college." I then ask, "In order to go to college, what do you have to do?" A typical answer is, "I have to pass high school." "How do you pass high school?" He concludes, "Well, I guess I have to write that paper." This scenario describes reaching a goal in a linear fashion.

Those on the spectrum can't piece things together unless we show them the logical steps in the progression. Now, that doesn't mean they will do all of their homework without question, but if you don't make it concrete by pointing out the connection in that linear fashion, it may not make any sense to them at all. This process has a similar effect of providing extrinsic motivators, but it works by projecting the outcomes so the child can see what's in it for them.

PLAN AHEAD

When my three daughters were very young, I would take them to the Rain Forest Café as a special treat. In order to maximize the possibility of success, I had a very specific way of handling the situation. We would start our day by eating an early breakfast so that we could arrive at the Café around 11:00 a.m., when it opened. That way, we did not have to wait to be seated.

The Café is located in the local mall. So, I would tell my girls, before ever leaving for the restaurant, that there would be no shopping. I set up their expectations in advance. I let them know that we would only be going for lunch and then coming straight back home. I would also tell them that we would not be buying anything at the Rain Forest Café gift shop before or after lunch. I was very explicit and thorough in my explanation of what "no shopping" meant. I did give them each five coins to throw into the alligator's mouth prior to eating lunch.

While we were driving to the Café, we would discuss my expectations of how they would act at the restaurant, as well as what we were going to order for lunch, so when we got there, we did not need a menu. In order to get served faster, I would order the food as they were showing us to our table. I asked the waitress to bring the bill with the

food, so there would be no wait when we were done eating. We wo
eat, pay the bill and be on our way in twenty minutes. Why did I do i
that way? To maximize the possibility of a successful outing. We always
had a good time!

Now, that type of plan isn't perfect; there can always be something
that comes up. One year, I thought my plan was running like clock-
work when one of the girls asked to use the restroom. Since I was a dad
out on my own with three young daughters, I took the girls into the
men's room with me to use the bathroom. It was a slight detour in my
plan, but it was easy to pull off because of all that I had set up prior to
going on the excursion.

Planning ahead works well with all children, but especially with
those on the spectrum who are much more successful if they have a
clear and accurate idea of what is coming up. By explaining expectations in as much detail as possible, you are setting up for success.

PROMPTING PRIOR

Motivating a child by rewarding him for the desired behavior, rather
than punishing him for the undesired behavior, works as long as the
prompting is prior. That means, spell out the boundaries in advance.
For example, "If you complete your homework, you can use the
computer for 15 minutes." Not clearly spelling out the conditions for
earning the reward before it is too late for the child to make an
informed choice will likely elicit responses such as, "I didn't know
that," or "That's not fair," or "You never said that." Again, you may
have felt that you didn't need to spell it out because, perhaps, it was
implied in the situation. But, as a result of his executive functioning
difficulties, the child was not able to connect the undesired outcome
to his behavior. That chain of events was not even on his radar screen.

To be effective, we need to be proactive and we need to react before
we get angry. If my own children are acting up, eventually, it will drive
me to the point when I'm going to do something about it. When my
three girls start to get surly, I'll remind them that they are heading
down a path that is going to get them in trouble and I'll say to them,
"If you keep this up, this is what the outcome will be."

oldest daughter preempts trouble with her sisters
hat is executive functioning. She can see that the
ʒ toward trouble and she makes a good choice not
it arrives. Individuals on the spectrum don't draw
vay; they don't have the foresight to make a good
choice based ⌐ ⌐utcome. So, as parents, teachers, and therapists, we
need to help them make better choices by presenting data in a way that
makes sense to them and prompting them before they actually get in
trouble. By projecting possible outcomes for them—by telling them
what will happen based on their choices—you can help them choose
the direction in which to proceed and the result they wish to create.

Motivation is a key factor that we sometimes overlook because we
might assume that the motivation in these individuals is intrinsic. I'm
not saying that there is no internal motivation that drives a child on the
spectrum, but it is different than for children not on the spectrum.
That's why being proactive and prompting prior works for them.

Now, the key is finding out what motivates your specific child.
What will make her want to work? I have found that the most effective
motivator is the child's time.

MY TIME AND YOUR TIME

My time and your time is a very straightforward concept. It is a social
skill. I talk, then you talk, then I talk, then you talk. If you always
dominate the conversation, then you won't have very many conversations because no one will want to talk to you. What my time and your
time means is doing something and thereby earning something.

Parents may punish their kids by taking away television or computer privileges. My preference would be to turn it around and make it
pertinent to the child. Tell him that if he does what he is supposed to
do, he will earn two hours of television or whatever else he may want
to do. That's exactly what we did with the boy who asked about the

social studies questions at the middle school. When that boy asked what was in it for him if he answered the five questions, the teacher told him he would get five minutes of free time at the end of the school day to do what he wanted to do. My time earns your time.

REWARD SPECIFIC BEHAVIOR

Years ago, when I started running groups for individuals with ASD, I wanted to teach children and adolescents on the spectrum the importance of asking questions of others based on what they said in conversation. In group, I would ask each child to "check in" and then I would try to get the others in the group to ask questions pertaining to what each said during check-in. Keep in mind that there are prerequisite skills that need to be in place before this can be accomplished, such as sitting without behaviors and listening to others. In one group, I had trouble getting them to ask questions of each other. I would say, "Tom, why don't you ask Pete about the trip he said he went on last weekend." Tom would say, "I don't care about Pete's trip over the weekend," which is a very common response for someone on the spectrum.

I decided to encourage the boys in this group to ask questions by providing external motivation; I promised them that I would have a pizza party for whichever of my groups asked the most questions during their group session. This particular group asked 180 questions in 45 minutes. It was humorous because, once they got into it, they would ask someone a question and then immediately look at me and say, "That is a question, Dr. Wahlberg, and it is worth a point." This is not a natural or intrinsic way to facilitate social interactions, but pizza worked as a motivator for these boys. Ultimately, it created habits that turned out to be good habits for inspiring questions in my group. Providing pizza as an incentive motivated them to do what they didn't want to do until it became a comfortable behavior that could be replicated socially.

Encourage the "Not-Having-to-Like-It-Just-Do-It" Attitude

Sometimes, parents will ask me, "Do I have to reward or bribe my child to get him to do anything that I want him to do?" I start by explaining that, to change their child's behavior over the long term, they may have to reward many things that they want their child to do in order to create good habits. Once those habits are formed, however, they can slowly start to modify the rewards for desired behavior to move the child more toward what would be considered normal, such as earning an allowance. Parents can also encourage their children to develop the not-having-to-like-it-just-do-it attitude that these kids will need in order to be functional in the larger world.

Making Choices

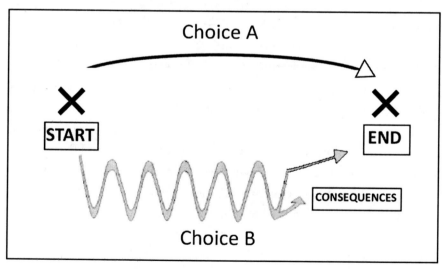

Diagram 15.1 – When a child is required to do something that he doesn't want to do (e.g., homework), he can choose path A and just get it done, or he can choose path B, procrastinating and fighting/arguing, which leads to unnecessary stress. Most kids realize that they have to do homework; this diagram illustrates that, either way, they will have to get it done, so why choose the more difficult path, one that could also lead to unpleasant consequences?

Building toward desired behavior without reward is the basis behind applied behavioral analysis (ABA) therapy. This therapy begins with providing a primary reinforcer for every occurrence of a behavior, then reducing the reinforcement to every 10th occurrence of the behavior, ultimately replacing the reward with social praise in place of the original reinforcer.

If you feel as if you are bribing your child, consider it the first step toward teaching your child how to do things she needs to do just because. With conscious effort, it is possible to transform that bribe into an understanding that we all need to do some things that we do not like to do.

SLOW DOWN AND RESPECT THEIR TIMING

Sometimes, we don't realize how long it takes for individuals on the spectrum to make sense of the information we present. In my first office, the entire back wall was covered in drawings that my clients had drawn and stuck on the wall. I encourage my clients to write or draw at the beginning of a session because it breaks the ice a little. As it happened, the kids would stick their pictures on my wall. One by one, they put the pictures up during therapy until the entire wall was covered. I called it "the wall of fame."

One day, I was in my office trying to teach a parent to understand how much time it takes a child with ASD for processing. I could tell that her son took some time to process, and that the mom was a little bit high strung. She felt that her son couldn't make choices no matter what she asked him.

I asked the boy if he wanted to use a pen or a pencil to draw a picture for the wall of fame. Of course, mom jumped in with, "He can't make decisions. He doesn't know how to…" I interjected, "Hold on. Let me just do this." I put the notepad on his lap and I held up a pen in one hand and a pencil in the other. I said, "Do you want a pen or a pencil?" Literally, right when those words came out of my mouth, mom said, "Well, he would probably use the pen. He would like the pen better. Why don't you just give him the pen?"

I stopped her again, "Just hold on. Let's give him a little time." I saw him looking at the pen, then the pencil, then the pen, then the pencil. Finally, after about 25 seconds, he grabbed the pen. Sometimes, we don't understand how long it takes them to process information. Remember, when they're young, they're not going to tell you that they don't understand and that they need you to slow down to give them time. They may be able to do that when they are adults but, as children, it's probably not going to happen.

So, in my office, I talk slower and usually ask the kids to explain what they are saying, or I ask them if I'm losing them in any way as we are talking. Allowing these kids the time they need to process can really improve results.

OFFER DIFFERENT PERSPECTIVES

Teach children to look at other variables, possibilities, or perspectives. This works hand-in-hand with stopping, thinking, and problem solving. Seeing other viable options can be hard for children on the spectrum, but they need to learn how to navigate an abstract world in order to be more flexible and functional in their daily lives. Throughout this book, I have provided numerous examples for parents and educators to help the ASD children in their care to learn how to move from rigid black and white thinking to somewhere in the middle—the abstract gray. Remember, the key is consistency and clarity; these children are smart, they just see the world very concretely. You can use that to your advantage by applying the techniques and treatments discussed in this chapter.

CHAPTER 16

STRATEGIES FOR EMOTIONAL REGULATION

For individuals with autism, being able to recognize when they are stuck is a milestone in their growth. Once they know how to determine if they are stuck, we can teach them strategies to get unstuck.

As the control theory suggests, the bodies of children with ASD are overwhelmed with the sensory environment, taking in too much sensory information at one time without an effective biological filter. Teaching a child on the spectrum how to regulate his own sensory system is one of the fundamentals in dealing with autism. Once individuals learn and apply this process of regulating their sensory systems, they then conserve neurological energy and are able to use that energy for higher level processing. Remember, these children are not neurologically hardwired to regulate themselves; this is a skill they must learn.

EMOTIONAL SELF-REGULATION STRATEGIES (FINDING THE GRAY)

After a child learns to regulate his sensory system, it becomes possible for him to become aware of himself on an emotional level. It is a monumental success when a child on the spectrum realizes what he is experiencing emotionally and is able to recognize subtle changes in his emotions. This is exciting for two reasons. First, this is an indicator that the child has broken out of the black and white thinking which had previously kept him stuck because so much of the data just didn't compute. He is now aware of the shades of gray in his emotions.

Second, once able to experience these subtleties in emotion, the possibility that he can make choices to move from one feeling to another appears; the door opens to growth, which was previously not possible if he consciously, or unconsciously, thought that he was a victim of his own emotional state, or that he could not control his own mind.

When a child with autism understands that it is possible for her to change emotionally, she can then learn to develop her skill in controlling her own mind. An effective way to develop this skill is to use a 0-10 point scale (or 0-3 or a 0-5 point scale for younger children) to teach them that they can actually quantify, in a black and white fashion, how they are feeling. This helps them learn to pay attention to their emotional changes as well as how to find the gray area, or middle ground, that can be elusive to them. Diagram 16.1 shows a simple chart that I use to illustrate an increasing volume of emotional intensity.

POINT SCALE TO MEASURE EMOTIONAL STATE

Diagram 16.1- A concrete visual representation like this 10-point scale can help a child on the spectrum identify and describe what he is feeling.

The terminology that a person with autism uses to describe how he feels can be much different from the terminology someone without autism would use. Often, a person with autism may use a term such as mad or sad to describe any emotional state that deviates from feeling okay. I find that anger is one of the most readily accessible emotions for individuals on the spectrum, therefore, it is easiest for them to describe and easiest for us to work with in therapy. Almost all individuals on the spectrum understand it quite well.

To help a child learn to evaluate his emotional level, I initially present a number scale to make sure that he understands what the numbers on the scale mean (which numbers are the biggest, smallest, etc.). When I feel certain that he understands the numbers on the scale, I establish the poles, i.e., the 0 and the 10 in terms of anger versus no anger. I clarify that "the most anger" is either 0 on the scale or 10 on the scale. Most children see the 0 equating to no anger at all and the 10 as very angry, or rage. Others see it the opposite way. Either way can work.

Then, I ask the child (many times with the help of parents) to describe an event that made her feel the most angry she has ever felt in her life. I continue, asking for a description of an event that made her feel no anger all, or completely happy. Of course, things are not always all or none when it comes to emotions, but when setting up a scale for emotions we must define the emotional state first by designating what the extremes mean, i.e., the poles (0 and 10), and then we can begin to explore the middle ground.

Let me give you an example. Recently, I was working with a young lady using this strategy. As we began, she told me that she never sees the middle between 0 and 10; she only sees things as black or white, all or none. I made sure she understood what the numbers represented on the scale. She said 0 would be no anger at all and 10 would represent the most anger she had ever felt. When I asked what event she recalled that would be classified in her mind as a 10, she said that her mom singing in the car on the way to my office was a 10. Both her mom and

I felt that this did not represent a 10; the young lady did not seem that upset by the event as she described it in my office.

After some thought, her mom remembered an incident when someone had accused her of hurting one of her cats. Her eyes got really big and I could see the emotion rising in her. They both agreed, "Yes that was a 10!" I noted that incident under the 10 on the scale. Then I asked her about an event that she would see as a 0, or something she does that she likes and causes no anger. She said watching her favorite shows on TV and eating cake. So I wrote that under the 0. After this, I placed the 0-10 chart in front of her and asked her what number would represent her mom singing in the car on the way to my office. She said, "Oh, my gosh, a 3 or a 4...I see the middle." It was almost instantaneous. She was able to experience the moderate nature of her feelings in relation to the two extremes.

The therapeutic value of an experience like this is that you are challenging the black and white way of thinking. When the individual establishes the poles, the extremes, and then you present data that is not extreme, she is able to see that an emotion can fall between her poles. She begins to see that all experience cannot be the same. Working with this chart helps individuals on the spectrum realize, sometimes for the first time in their lives, that there is a middle ground.

Using the child's own experience, rather than words that are meaningless to her, is the key. In the future, this young lady will be able to use the scale and evaluate an event at a 10 in contrast to other situations, thus giving her an emotional benchmark. She will no longer say that every difficult experience is ranked a 10. She cannot, because that data no longer computes. Her mom singing in the car is not equal to her being accused of hurting her cats. While this strategy is an effective way to begin to erode black and white or all-or-none thinking, and this 0-10 chart exercise enables these children to see a middle ground that was previously nonexistent to them, every child is different. Not every child has an immediate shift like the young lady in my example above.

For children with autism who are nonverbal, or who are very young, we can quantify their emotional state with concrete visual aides like a thermometer that moves up and down, with the color red representing the changes in emotional state. I met a family recently that used volcano pictures. The first picture had no lava. The lava from the volcano increased until the volcano had completely erupted. Similarly, one can also use pictures of the child very upset at one end of the scale and the child happy at the other end. Keep in mind that the poles need to be established based on the child's actual experience, not on emotional language that might not be meaningful (i.e., happy or sad).

Another child with whom I worked liked electricity, and he used a visual that involved surges of electricity, with the strongest surge representing the most anger. Here is a diagram that I have used for nonverbal or younger kids:

HOW I FEEL RIGHT NOW

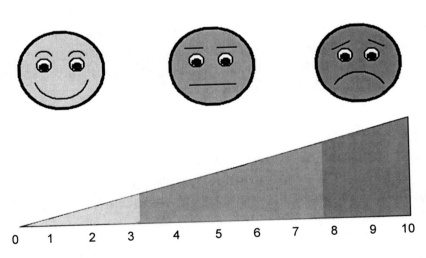

Diagram 16.2 - This diagram can be used for younger or nonverbal children who have difficulty expressing how they feel.

There are programs designed for little ones with autism that use visual systems to teach them about emotional states; one example is "How Does Your Engine Run?" We just need to be careful that the younger children are able to understand what our language means, for instance, "running fast," or "running slow," or "running just right." How do we know that they understand what these phrases mean? This is why asking the child to describe an event and share his own experience becomes so important in providing a baseline to understand how that child makes sense of the scale.

Once we can get kids on the spectrum to acknowledge their own emotional states, we are then able to teach strategies to monitor and manage those emotions. We can help them learn to recognize when they start to feel themselves becoming upset, (e.g., angry, sad, hungry, etc.) and how to address the issue before they are off the charts emotionally. At that point, it may be too late to do anything preventative, so you may just have to wait out the emotional storm.

The same 0-10 scale I just described can also be used to prepare an individual with ASD prior to entering into a situation that may be challenging for her to handle. Using this scale can help the child identify where she is emotionally, which could reduce a great deal of emotional discomfort in the midst of the situation.

MANAGING THE TENDENCY TO OVERREACT

This same technique, identifying and measuring emotions through a visual tool, can be used to manage a tendency to overreact to any situation. I worked with a young man whose mother said that he overreacts to the slightest things at home. When I asked for an example, she described an incident that had occurred on the previous night when she asked her son if he had remembered to brush his teeth. He was not in any trouble; she just asked. The mom explained to me that he had forgotten, but she expressed concern that his emotional response was very intense. He had a terrible meltdown.

I used the 0-10 chart in this situation. He was familiar with the chart and had previously used it to regulate his anger. I asked him to use the chart to describe "doing something bad." So, in this case, a 10 would represent the worst thing he could do; he gave the example, robbing a bank. The 0 represented something good he could do, and he said, "Helping an old lady cross the street."

When I put the chart in front of him and asked him what number he thought forgetting to brush his teeth represented, he looked at the chart for quite some time, and finally said, "Probably a 1 or a 2." His mother and I agreed. I then asked him what number he thought his reaction to the situation had been the night before. He admitted it was a 10. He was starting to evaluate the situation and how he responded in terms of both a good and bad continuum. Prior to this point, he viewed everything as either all good or all bad. Remember Diagram 7.1 depicting black and white thinking? With the help of this 0-10 scale, this young man was beginning to see the possibility of something between the two extremes. Recognizing that a middle ground (the gray area) exists is a prerequisite to being there emotionally.

CALMING DOWN IS A CHOICE

I like to teach individuals on the spectrum that they are able to not only recognize changes in their emotional state, but that they also have a choice about how they respond. They can choose to calm themselves down, or they can choose not to. If they choose to calm down, they can use their strategies to do so. Strategies may include things like taking sensory breaks, using the sensory backpack, counting to 10, doing breathing exercises, using positive self-talk, etc. I find it is not so much about what strategy they use as it is about recognizing the change in emotion and realizing that they have a choice about getting upset or controlling their emotional state. Once that happens, any strategy they use can be effective.

On the next page is a diagram that I use to show the choice they can make to calm themselves.

STRATEGIES TO HELP CALM THE BRAIN

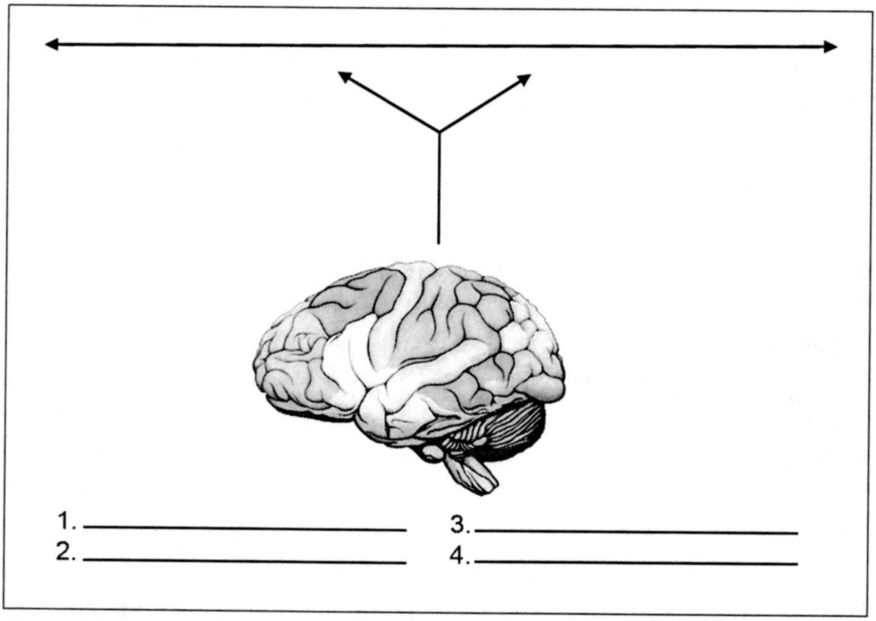

1. _____   3. _____
2. _____   4. _____

Diagram 16.3 - By listing possible strategies that might help a child calm down, the individual learns to understand that he can make positive choices to prevent anger from escalating.

I tell the individual that this diagram represents his brain and the line coming from the top of the brain represents when he starts to think about something that may be upsetting. When he gets to the middle of the Y, or the crossroads, he can make a choice about which way he wants to go. I usually put the 0-10 chart above this diagram. So, on one side you have no anger and on the other side you have a high degree of anger. I tell the individual that he can choose to not get angry and use strategies to calm himself. I list possible strategies under the diagram (where the numbers 1–4 are shown).

You can use this concept to help teach a child to control his emotional states, from anger to anxiety, as well as to help him focus and learn appropriate responses to uncomfortable or difficult situations. The goal is to help the child avoid the auto-escalation that can happen when he associates other memories.

AUTO-ESCALATION/ASSOCIATING MEMORIES

Children on the spectrum are not hardwired to avoid being upset; their systems seem to naturally get sucked into uneasy feelings or unrest. Remember that they are visual thinkers. Often, when they begin to feel an emotion, they very quickly get a visual of events they have experienced in the past that elicited the same feeling. This compounds the emotion they are currently experiencing and leads to a seemingly automatic escalation in feeling. This may be the reason that an autistic child can go from 0 to 10 on the anger scale very quickly. Diagram 16.4 illustrates the connection.

This diagram helps me to explain to parents how individuals on the spectrum tap into a wellspring of anxiety. All of the prior incidents may not be connected in any other way, except that they created a certain feeling. When the child experiences that same feeling again, the emotion intensifies because it brings back the memories of when she felt that way before.

ANXIETY TRIGGERS FROM PAST EXPERIENCES

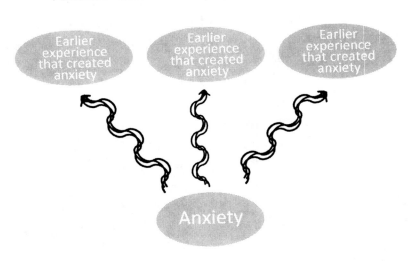

Diagram 16.4 -- People on the autistic spectrum are visual thinkers; an event that upsets them can trigger thoughts of past events they have experienced that have caused the same emotion. They remember and visualize these past experiences, which creates more anxiety. The problem is then compounded because they not only feel the current emotions, but they relive the earlier events.

Those of us without ASD can tune this out; we do not think about all other events that elicited the same emotion. While we are able to manage this type of mental association, children with ASD do not have a filter that says, "Don't go there—think about something different." There is a snowball effect; once the ball starts rolling it just keeps going, and these children can wind up inordinately distressed because of the memories of a previous experience.

If, at that critical moment when their minds begin to go down this path and they become agitated, they can apply some simple strategies, they can break the escalation pattern and calm themselves. Strategies such as using a visual system, writing an outline of steps to follow, or recalling memorized lists are very effective calming tools in this situation.

Trying to create those tools in the moment is very unsuccessful, so they need to be ready in advance. Most children with ASD need help to develop a list of options from which to draw upon when they need to calm down. Keep in mind that their neurological systems do not do this naturally, so they need to be taught. For little ones, under the age of 5 or 6, who are not yet reading, we use pictures. Creating that picture list will probably require input from parents or teachers in addition to information from the young child.

It is so important that we help them learn to break the pattern of getting angry and going immediately from 0 to 10. As you can imagine, controlling anger is a life lesson that increases functionality dramatically. These visual tools, when they are working effectively, remind the child to catch himself before he escalates to an extreme. With this awareness, children with ASD can start the process of calming down before it's too late, and they can effectively stop the auto-escalation.

I teach kids to identify the critical point at which to use these strategies in order to calm themselves. By recognizing when they start to get emotionally charged, they can apply these tools when they are at

5 or 6 on the scale, rather than waiting until they are at 10. Remember the earlier description given by a man with autism who explained how difficult it was to change his train of thought once his mind started to go in a certain direction? Being able to call a time out in that compulsive emotional landslide is a very useful skill, one that will dramatically improve the child's flexibility and functionality.

BREAKING THE CYCLE

Another strategy that I use when individuals on the spectrum are getting stuck, or fixated, on something is one I call "breaking the cycle." I teach these individuals to stop themselves from perseverating (obsessing) on a topic by doing something that distracts them from their obsessive thoughts. I use the following diagram to help them visualize what I am talking about.

The goal is to empower individuals on the spectrum to learn to control their emotions. These individuals typically strive to control situations; this diagram allows them to identify how they control their thinking and hyperfocus in a way that will help them become more functional. In the middle circle, the individual writes what he might be obsessing about. In the outer circles, he writes the strategies he can use to break that obsessive thought or cycle. This chart should be prepared when the child is calm—in therapy or at home—and reviewed or practiced often enough so that when a situation arises, he is capable of using the practiced strategies to break the cycle.

In many cases, individuals on the spectrum seem to need another person to break the cycle (usually the mom). They are unable to calm themselves on their own, unless they are taught how to do so. A common pattern is to push mom to the point at which she gets really mad, which seems to break the cycle. It is as if the child on the spectrum realizes that mom is officially done and, interestingly enough, the cycle stops. Sometimes they get angry if she cannot fix the problem with which they are struggling.

BREAKING THE CYCLE CHART

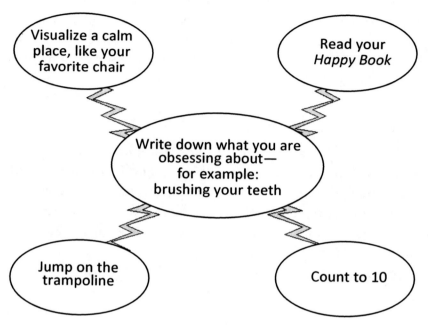

Diagram 16.5 - This chart helps children to identify strategies they can use to calm themselves when they begin to get obsessive about something. It is a good idea to work on this chart when the child is calm.

I frequently see the mom act as the lightening rod for an individual on the spectrum. The controlled emotion needs to vent and individuals on the spectrum want to do so in the safest environment, which is home. They keep it together in school, and when they get home the emotion is expressed in full force, and usually the mom is the one who attracts that energy.

The same pattern occurs when it comes to doing homework. In some cases, individuals on the spectrum are stuck, unable to organize themselves enough to do homework on their own. They can only do homework if someone is sitting with them. This chart helps them to break the cycle and to be able to self-organize.

STRATEGIES TO AVOID GETTING STUCK

For individuals with autism, being able to recognize when they are stuck is a milestone in their growth. Once they know how to determine if they are stuck, we can teach them strategies to get unstuck. First, they need to be calm. Until they are in a state of calm, there is no point being in a classroom, or engaging in social situations, since, at that moment, they can't process or absorb what is going on because they are too distracted by the stimulus around them.

Without some intervention, individuals with autism can get stuck thinking about negative events and spiral downward emotionally without being able to let it go (see the section on auto-escalation on page 176). It is crucial that they learn to recognize changes in their emotional state before they are at the end of their scale. When an individual is at the intense end of the scale, it is very difficult (if not impossible) to change his thought process. These individuals can also easily get stuck in not doing things that they are asked to do, such as chores or homework, for example. They just do not want to do the activity (times 10), and they get stuck, unable to move themselves forward.

Here is a typical scenario where the individual is stuck: A young man with Asperger's disorder was recently in my office because he really struggled doing assignments for which he could not see the relevance. When I met him, his grades were C's and D's, although he is a very bright student. The first fall we worked together, he was able to dramatically improve his grades because he decided to do the work. He ran into trouble in the spring, when he had a literature class; he decided to skim the 400-page book instead of reading it and to ignore the assigned study guides because they were not going to be graded. However, the teacher did encourage the class to complete the guides because students would be allowed to refer to them during the test.

Well, needless to say, the test did not go very well for this young man; he was totally unprepared. We spoke about what happened and he was sure it would never happen again. When school started the following term, there was another book to read and more study guides to be completed. Once again, these study guides were not going to be scored, but could be used for the test. Guess what happened? He did not complete the study guides. His father was livid and fumed, "How could he have not learned his lesson?" I explained that he was stuck at the point of not doing something that he did not want to do since it was not graded. He could not get himself to do it. This is a perfect example of how individuals with autism behave; once their brains start in a direction, it is difficult to stop the momentum or change direction. Doing something in a different way is extremely difficult, if not impossible, for them.

To help that young man overcome being stuck, I had him write himself a script to read each night before he does homework. This is what he wrote:

How to Get Unstuck Paper:

"Think about something positive/some kind of reward/something to look forward to after I get this task accomplished. Also, think: "how will this benefit me in the long run?" If it's studying for a test, I will get an A, which will get me a better grade in class, which will increase my GPA, which will help me get into college, which will help my education and get me a job, which is what I will do for a decent part of my life."

OTHER STRATEGIES TO MANAGE EXTREME BEHAVIOR

Given the tendency for individuals with autism to wear their hearts on their sleeves (that is, to be very blunt about what they are feeling), it is not a difficult stretch to understand that their behavior can also be perceived as blunt or extreme. From the outside, they seem either okay or very bad. We don't often see a middle range of emotion in them. Parents usually describe a lack of emotion which, in this context is a good state. That absence of emotion is contrasted with upset, which can manifest as yelling, aggression, tantrums, or even rage. Both the child and his parents can benefit from the ability to recognize subtle changes in emotions before it's too late, and have a plan available to interrupt the pattern. Below are additional options for intervention:

PRACTICE IN ADVANCE

Sometimes an individual with autism will describe a situation that creates such turmoil and duress for him that he feels he cannot be effective at using the scale technique, or any other, in the moment. Many of the situations that threaten to feel overwhelming involve social interactions. My experience suggests that if the child is concerned that he will be overwhelmed by a situation, he is most likely correct. Intervention needs to focus on practicing the situation in advance, in an effort not to end up trying to do it in the moment. This is most effectively done in a place that is nonthreatening, such as at home, in a therapist's office, or at school.

With practice, an abstract unknown becomes more concrete and, therefore, more manageable. Unfortunately, it is impossible to predict the future, so this advance practice cannot cover every possibility for whatever events they might encounter. Remember the young man who was practicing a phone call to join in a group? When the receptionist asked him to "Please hold," and that response was not one of his anticipated scenarios, he was unable to continue the call.

The act of practicing is important. In my groups, we practice small talk, which can be problematic since most social interactions do not follow the same pattern every time. For example, slang can make the exchange confusing. I treated an adult who drove his own car, lived alone next door to his sister, and had a job as a maintenance man at a toy store. He expressed his confusion one day over a common greeting, asking me, "Why would someone say, 'What's up?'" He went on to say that he answered with, "The lights, the ceiling tiles..." Unable to grasp the meaning of this colloquialism, he wondered why a person would ask him such a thing.

This same young man was on his way home from his maintenance job when his favorite car got a flat tire. He liked his car because of the "hum it made as it drove across the road." Unfortunately, when he got that flat tire, he pulled into a Cadillac dealership and ended up driving away in a brand new Escalade. Why? Because the man at the dealership told him that he needed a new car and he took that literally. There lies the difficulty for someone with a social disability in a world that, unfortunately, has many predators (not that all car dealers are predators).

In addition to all the other stumbling blocks, the individual's need for additional processing time may impact how a social interaction goes. Practice may help reduce the processing time in an actual situation. Although practice can be a very effective strategy in many circumstances, it cannot cover the myriad number of possibilities in any one social encounter. Here is another strategy that can truncate the number of possibilities and help the individual with ASD manage the direction of a social interaction—using written messages.

PRE-WRITTEN MESSAGES TO EDUCATE OTHERS

Under duress, it may be more effective to utilize a strategy that does not involve the individual with ASD having to explain herself verbally or calm herself down (which may be impossible in that moment). This strategy would require educating those involved in the situation about what the individual with autism is experiencing and why. This can be very helpful in steering an encounter to a successful conclusion.

For example, individuals with autism may come into contact with police officers, for whatever reason. Many neuro-typical people are uncomfortable around law enforcement officials; think about how it feels when a police car is behind you while you're driving. For an individual with autism, this can be stressful times 10. If the individual with autism happens to be an adolescent, he may fall victim to a certain stigma attached to teenagers in general. That might be even further compounded by the fact that adolescents (who are discovering a sense of autonomy and feeling as though they are adults) think that they understand how the world operates. Now we have all the makings of a potential problem.

If a police officer approaches an individual with autism and begins to talk to him, the stress of this could cause the teen to go into shutdown mode and render him unable to respond to the officer. How do you suppose this looks to the police? The individual may even smile due to nervousness, which might be perceived by the officer as arrogance or rudeness. Obviously, if the police officer misinterprets the response of the individual, the situation could escalate.

If this individual with autism could hand the police officer a pre-written note that read:

> Hi, my name is Tom Smith and I have Asperger's disorder. I often get very nervous in social situations and have trouble coming up with words to say and to communicate what I am thinking and feeling. It takes me a few minutes to process what is going on when I am nervous. Could you please allow me a few minutes to communicate with you what I am feeling and thinking? If you have questions could you please call my mother, father or doctor at the following numbers? Thanks for your patience.

This could potentially diffuse a situation that could get very serious very quickly, especially if the police officer begins to get physical and the individual begins to resist or fight back.

Here's an example of an interesting encounter with the police that stemmed from the innocent, yet quirky, behavior of one of my clients. I had just started working with a young man who was driving to my office by himself. He was obsessed with hitting the exact speed limit each time he started driving from a complete stop. He would start at 0 and expect to hit 45 miles per hour immediately when starting out. If he felt that he was over or under 45, he would completely stop his car and start over.

One day, on his way to my office, he did this stopping and starting maneuver. Another driver phoned the police, and an officer was dispatched to pull him over. Once pulled over, my client became overloaded and felt like the officer was taking too long to handle the situation, so he began to drive away. Needless to say, the officer did not respond very well to this obvious sign of disrespect. He actually dove into my client's car and turned it off. What do you suppose happened when he touched my client? To make a long story short, this young man ended up strapped to a gurney and taken to the emergency room.

If this young man had presented a pre-written statement to explain his situation to the officer, the ensuing events might have gone easier on everyone concerned. He needed to learn to manage his emotions in order to handle situations such as this. What we worked on therapeutically was how he could calm himself down when he felt stressed. Once I taught him how to regulate his emotional state, he was better able to manage himself in situations where he felt uncomfortable or uneasy.

I also know of parents who carry pre-preprinted cards similar to business cards explaining that their child has autism. Then, if a disturbance occurs in a public place, the parent can easily and efficiently explain to others that their child has special needs and is not being mistreated.

INTERVENING AT THE POINT OF AN EMOTIONAL MELTDOWN

I often get asked how to intervene when a child is at a 10, at the height of a tantrum. The unfortunate reality is that there is little we can do once kids get there, so preventing them from getting there is the best strategy. If they do end up in a meltdown, all we can do as parents, therapists, or educators is to keep them safe from physical harm and get them to a place where they can calm themselves down. Once they are at a 10, they often do not want to use "any stupid strategies," so we need to wait it out. That is why I advocate recognizing and managing emotional states before the children hit extremes. Prevention is the best strategy to avoid meltdowns.

DEVELOPING THEIR ABILITY TO READ THE EMOTIONS OF OTHERS

The same qualities that make it tough for people with autism to read their own emotions also make it difficult to read the emotions of others; it is a skill that usually needs to be taught. This is an area where visual tools can be very effective. First, with the help of a number scale, a child can learn to identify the intensity of her own emotions (1-10 for older kids, 0-5 or even 0-3 for the little ones). Because many of these children seem to go from 0 to 10 with no stops in between, practicing this technique also helps them to see the middle of the emotional range. Then, once they understand how to use this tool to identify their own emotions, they can use it to help them begin to read the emotions of other people.

One other tool I use in treatment for younger kids is a "Happy Book." This is a book that the child has put together with pictures or visuals that make her happy and distract her from whatever is going on. I usually use a scrapbook that has one picture per page. Often these pictures include family pets, photos of trips or activities the child has enjoyed, video games, cards, or her favorite drawings. The interesting thing about black and white thinking is that one cannot feel like a 10 and a 0 at the same time. If children learn to control their brains in a way to focus on things that they like (analogous to 0 on the scale), they cannot feel like a 10 at the same time. When they are somewhere in between, it is good because it is manageable. You can talk and deal with a child who is at a 5 as opposed to a 10; a child can process and make sense of things at a 5, where he is seemingly out of control at a 10.

PROVIDING MOTIVATION: "WHAT'S IN IT FOR ME?"

Motivation is always an integral part of every intervention for a child on the spectrum. Remember that children on the spectrum need to be extrinsically motivated. Again, to someone with ASD, it is all about, "What's in it for me?"

Many individuals do not see anything wrong with their behavior or the way that they handle their emotions, so they will not change on their own. Taking action because they know it will help them requires intrinsic motivation. Even if they know a strategy helps them, they may not use it. Therefore, we need to provide motivation to coax them to use the strategies. Motivation is always a key factor when trying to modify behavior of someone on the spectrum.

CHAPTER 17

USING STRUCTURE IN TREATMENT

When we as parents, teachers, and therapists use consistent language, consistent visual systems, and consistent rules to emphasize the sameness in the message, the child has a stable reference point that he can rely on to steady him during transitions.

I f we establish structured, consistent programming across settings (home, school, therapy, etc.), we provide individuals on the spectrum an opportunity to develop a sense of confidence, control, and comfort in the consistency of their world. This continuity in treatment is very important. The consistency also optimizes the likelihood that they will generalize what they have learned, which means that they will apply information learned in one context appropriately to a different context. Being able to generalize is a very important life skill. Therefore, the more consistent, the more black and white the environment, the more easily understood that environment becomes as it reduces doubt and confusion and works with the child's black and white linear processing. By establishing continuity, we're creating an environment that makes sense to them.

ESTABLISH ROUTINE, THEN CHANGE IT

This consistency in the environment builds a framework that makes the process of adapting to new situations easier for the child. That is to say, when parents, teachers, and therapists use consistent language, consistent visual systems, and consistent rules to emphasize the sameness in the message, the child has a stable reference point that he can rely on to steady him during transitions.

When this uniformity does not exist at home, in school, and in therapy, kids on the spectrum can often fly under the radar. They can easily manipulate their world to avoid what is uncomfortable. Usually, they meet with some success until something happens that uncovers them. For example, if parents and teachers don't communicate effectively, a middle school student can tell parents that his homework is done and get away with it—until report cards go home. At that point, it is often too late to intervene and change the outcome.

Once we have successfully created a surrounding environment that is black and white, we can begin to make shifts to change it. For example, as soon as I help a teacher to effectively employ the visual systems, use schedules, be structured, be consistent, etc., and the teacher says, "Hey, it's going great! Little Joey is doing well. His behavior is under control," then I get a big smile on my face and I say, "Okay, now we have to change things. Something little, but we have to change something!" We have to teach these kids how to deal with change. That's part of the process.

The change can be as simple as altering the visual schedule in an early childhood classroom. For example, if we regularly provide a picture schedule of the day's activities, once the routine is established and understood, we can modify one activity during the day. As long as the routine of the daily schedule is established, individuals do much better when an adjustment is introduced; they can look at the daily activities and have the opportunity to prepare mentally and to visualize the change, eliminating the discomfort of a surprise.

Individuals on the spectrum are able to use their linear thinking to frame the change, knowing that the activities happening before and after the new activity are still going to be the same. Using this type of systematic approach takes away the ambiguity (and thus the fear, stress, and discomfort) that can accompany change for these kids. By stretching their flexibility in this controlled way, we work toward bringing the kids closer to seeing the shades of gray. Providing the individual with the lead time he needs to process the change is also very important to the success of this method.

STRUCTURE PROVIDED BY BOUNDARIES

Parenting is a tough, nonstop job when your child is on the spectrum. As a result of their way of processing the world, these children are constantly testing the boundaries. I treated one eighth-grade boy who continually lied about doing his homework. He would try over and over again to avoid doing his homework, and he always got caught lying.

One day in therapy, in an attempt to understand why he continued to lie about his homework, I asked him if he could remember the last time he had lied without getting caught. Recalling exactly when it was, he immediately responded, "Third grade, Mrs. Johnson, math problems 1-28." I was astounded. He has been caught lying about his homework for five years, yet he still keeps trying to get away with it. I asked him why in the world he would continue, and his reply was, "Because there's always a chance."

Some children on the spectrum are constantly checking to see if the boundaries are in place. It can be calming to them when they see the boundary is still there.

Here is another example of testing the boundaries. In the movie *Jurassic Park*, there is a scene where the security director of the park is giving a tour to the two scientists who had been invited to the island. When they approach the velociraptor holding pen, the security director, describing the intelligence of these creatures, explains that the electric fence surrounding the pen is charged with 10,000 volts of power and that all of the other dinosaurs had learned, after being shocked once, that the fence is electrified, so they steer clear of it. He explains that the velociraptors also had experienced the shocks from the fence, they know that the fence is electrified, yet they test the fence every day to make sure that it is turned on. Every day they think that this might be the day that the fence is not turned on! Just like some children on the spectrum.

One of the keys to effective intervention is the establishment of very clear, consistent, black and white boundaries, or rules. The most successful children I treat have parents who set definite boundaries and then teach their children to navigate within those restrictions. I set very high standards for the children I treat. These are smart kids and they can follow rules. I do not expect them to understand and follow every social convention, but they can learn to follow simple rules. That is what is required to survive in the world, and I want them to learn that skill so they can be functional and happy.

The earlier we set these boundaries, the better the children learn to adapt and function within them. It is hard for parents of neuro-typical children to set boundaries, but it is very important. Many times, I find that it is even harder for parents with exceptional children to set boundaries. However, when your child has an exceptionality like autism, it is even more important to set and maintain strict boundaries, especially when enforcing them sets off tantrums or other problem behaviors designed to manipulate the situation. All kids need to learn to cope when they don't get what they want.

The school environment can be a very good place for an individual with ASD if the environment is structured and consistent, which is often the case. School can be a place where the routine and schedule, teacher and principal, etc., remain consistent over time. Lunch, for example is always at the same time, unless there is a special day. The teacher does not say, "Lunch is usually at noon, but I think today we will not go until 12:10." By its very nature, school is scheduled and regimented.

The difficulty with the school environment is that, while school systems establish rules and boundaries extensively, the children are not always taught how to navigate within those boundaries. For individuals without ASD who can read social clues, learn the ropes from friends, generalize concepts, or are simply very flexible in the moment, this does not pose a problem. They can learn, adapt, and integrate into the school's structure. For individuals with ASD, however, the inability to adapt or learn from their experiences is part of their exceptionality, which can make understanding and managing within the boundaries difficult; it can pose a big problem.

TEACH THE CHILD TO NAVIGATE BOUNDARIES APPROPRIATELY

Individuals without autism have the ability naturally to figure out the rules and boundaries on their own or with the help of their peers. In many cases, individuals with autism may find it difficult just to self-regulate their internal emotions and calm themselves down, let alone discern the rules. If we set up rules for classroom behavior, but do not teach these individuals how to handle the rules, we set them up to fail, in many cases.

It is important that a child on the spectrum not only knows the boundaries so that he can try to work within them, but also knows when he needs an exception and how to appropriately ask for that exception. For example, one boundary at school is that you sit in your seat quietly. The child needs to know that this is what he is supposed to do, but he also needs to have the tools to manage himself if he is becoming overwhelmed by sitting in his seat.

A child on the spectrum needs an appropriate way to communicate her distress before she hits meltdown. Teaching her this is teaching her to navigate the boundaries. I have already described the break card as a technique for indicating the need for a break (see Chapter 15, Treatment and Techniques). This is one way of requesting to see the social worker or requesting permission to do some other prearranged modification in order to manage or control the sense of being overwhelmed.

Here are some ways to help teach a child to navigate within the boundaries. We need to utilize these different methods in order to increase the child's learning and level of functioning:

1. *Provide rewards and consequences.* Children with ASD need to have clear expectations of what is in it for them. Provide two choices: if (A), then this will happen; if (B), then this will happen, and then follow through. Give them a chance to think about their choices and outcomes prior to making a decision or performing the action.

2. *Explain that they don't have to like it, they just have to do it.* This is an essential life skill. I say this all the time in my practice. I never try to convince individuals on the spectrum to like the activity, I simply reaffirm that they just have to do it, even while not liking it. For example, going to school, or emptying the dishwasher.

3. *Teach problem solving.* Teach them how to problem solve various situations. Teach them to stop and think about other options in any given situation. I worked with a young man who was meeting his friends in the pool at the local park. He arrived at the park and looked in the pool, and his friends were not "in the pool," so he went to the payphone to call his mother to come get him. He did not problem solve the situation on any level. When we worked on this in therapy, I asked him to come up with three possible scenarios of where his friends could have been and then three possible things he could have done to find them. As a result, he began to learn to problem solve.

4. *Use concrete facts to explain boundaries.* Break down the information into concrete facts. Remove the abstract and present black and white data whenever possible. A boundary that exists just because is difficult for those on the spectrum to manage; facts and data presented clearly and concretely are appropriate. Use lists, numbers, and diagrams whenever possible.

5. *Encourage them to practice.* We need to teach individuals with ASD how to understand and accept boundaries—through practice. As I stated earlier, this is done more effectively when they can practice in a moment when they are not stressed or under duress. We can plan out various scenarios and write scripts for them to practice.

Again, I have very high expectations for kids on the spectrum when it comes to boundaries and following rules. That being said, some expectations do need to be modified when it comes to their social abilities.

CHAPTER 18

TEACHING SOCIAL SKILLS

Developing appropriate social skills is paramount for individuals on the spectrum. There is a comfort level that individuals need to feel in order to be able to process and understand what is happening socially.

*D*eveloping appropriate social skills is paramount for individuals on the spectrum. There is a comfort level that individuals need to feel in order to be able to process and understand what is happening socially. They need to be at that level of comfort to be receptive to learning in a social setting. The benefit of working in a group is that it allows the participants to practice and learn in a real social setting, one in which they can experience that level of comfort.

SOCIAL GROUPS

When I am forming a social group, I like to meet each child individually to make sure that he will benefit from the group setting and to determine which group would be the best fit. I explain how the group runs, the schedule, and some of my expectations. With the younger children, I may need to teach some prerequisite skills individually prior to their participation in the group. With older children (ages 9 and up), more than likely they have been a part of a group in the school setting, so they understand the process.

I tell them that my expectation is that they will sit in a chair (unless they need a break), they will listen to me and follow my directions, and they will respect others in the group. Respecting others in the group may be something that needs some explanation. If so, I explain that, to begin with, only one person talks at a time, and that we take turns talking in group. I begin by teaching children and adolescents to sit and listen to what others are saying in group.

We often play games to see who can remember what others have said during the group. We start by having each child check in, discussing what he has been doing the last couple of weeks, and sharing if he has anything interesting coming up in the near future. I then try to teach the children to ask questions related to what each person said during her turn to check in. This is a process, and it can take time to develop. Eventually, the kids do learn to take turns and listen to each other.

In the group setting, the members determine the rate of progress for the entire group. We take steps in a progression. Once they are comfortable listening and asking pertinent questions, the children practice engaging in small talk with each other. When they can perform these activities, many children begin to describe difficult situations they have encountered since their last visit. It is very powerful when we begin role-playing these situations within the group. Then I can teach in the moment, with situations that mean something to the children in the group.

Typically, in my practice, groups are together for 12 to 18 months. It takes time for the individuals in these groups to get comfortable, learn the skills I am teaching, and establish meaningful friendships. Many of my group members will tell me that their only friends are in their group. Over the years, I have actually held a number of birthday parties in my groups. We share cake, ice cream, and gift bags in my office during group because the kids I see are not usually invited to parties and are not comfortable with inviting kids from their class to a party (because, all too often, when they do invite peers to an event, those kids don't show up).

I work with some college-age individuals who had been together in a group during high school for as long as three to four years. They will periodically call and ask me when their social group will meet next, because they want to attend. Most importantly, they will call each other outside of group and get together.

Based on my experience, high-functioning individuals on the spectrum have the ability to carry on a basic conversation in a one-on-one setting, especially with adults, but they become overloaded when engaging with peers. The adults are usually more compassionate and patient, while peers are less apt to accommodate the individual who can't keep up in the conversation. One client summed it up for me. He said that he could see how much fun it would be to be in a social setting, but that he "gets so nervous and has trouble talking with others." Remember, times 10.

SOCIAL SCRIPTS

Social scripts are a good example of taking something very complex and flexible and making it more concrete. In a social script, an individual with ASD is given a short series of steps to follow in a certain context. For example:

To Greet Someone:

1) Say, "Hello."

2) Extend your hand.

3) Ask, "How are you today?"

The difficulty with the social script is that the nuances that apply to each story change, which can create anxiety and difficulty for individuals with ASD. This is not to say that social scripts are not extremely important in treatment, but they need to be carefully written because of the ambiguity that social situations present.

CHAPTER 19

COPING WITH OTHER LIFE ISSUES

I will tell you, with a child on the spectrum, you have to
pick your battles. You cannot deal with every issue at once.
You have to stay focused on what is most important.

Because of the complexities of any human relationship, it is no surprise that individuals with autism spectrum disorder face many challenges when trying to build and maintain friendships. These challenges are diagnostic and clinically significant for them and, again, this is part of what separates those on the spectrum from those not on the spectrum.

FRIENDSHIP AND RELATIONSHIP CHALLENGES

When evaluating a child, I look for signs that peer relationships are a challenge. Does the child go to birthday parties? Does he get invited to the homes of friends for play dates and overnights? Is he able to manage group interactions and play? Is she always picked last for team events, or excluded from group activities? Does she have trouble in school with projects that require group participation?

Individuals on the spectrum will often interact reasonably well with older individuals and younger individuals, but they will struggle with social interactions involving peers. A child on the spectrum who is playing ball with a bunch of other kids may find it difficult to adapt to special rules because, in her mind, "this isn't the way the game is played." In other words, the child may not be flexible enough to adopt adjustments to the rules in order to be part of the group.

For example, let's say that there are not enough players to field two separate baseball teams. The individuals playing may decide that because there are not enough players, they are not going to have a right fielder. So, they adopt the rule that if you hit the ball to right field, you are "out." The child on the spectrum may have an issue with this change to the rules. If she is playing with a group of older children, the more mature kids may just acquiesce to the child on the spectrum to keep the peace. If there are younger children playing, they may just agree with the older child on the spectrum because she is older. The age difference makes it possible for the child on the spectrum to control the rules or the situation. The problem occurs when her same-aged peers (who do not agree with the child on the spectrum) are neither willing to acquiesce nor make an exception. In many cases, the child on the spectrum will quit—she will not play because she cannot be flexible enough to accept the new rule that hitting the ball to right field will result in an out.

Another social difference that I sometimes see is that boys on the spectrum like to hang out with the girls, and girls on the spectrum like to hang out with the boys. This may be because boys on the spectrum tend to be uncoordinated and do not generally like or play sports, whereas girls on the spectrum sometimes really like rough and tumble play and do not do well chatting with other girls. This reversal of the typical roles is an interesting phenomenon. It is not necessarily a bad thing, however, it can have negative ramifications. If, for instance, a child does not establish a core group of friends of the same gender, it could create a social void for the child. I encourage kids on the spectrum, especially those who are extroverted, to build friendships with other kids who are of the same gender.

With all the social difficulties that children on the spectrum experience, friendships are almost always a challenge. This challenge is one that some children simply don't have the desire or motivation to work through, thus many children with autism end up spending much of their time alone. Parents should encourage their children by setting up play dates. As with anything you plan for these black and white thinking kids, provide a structured and specific schedule for how the play date will unfold. For example: from 1:00 to 1:20, the children will play a board game; from 1:20 to 1:30, they will have a snack; from 1:30 to 2:00, they will play on the swings; at 2:00, the other child will go home. As your child becomes accustomed to having other children over, you can increase the time. I discuss this further on page 209.

DEALING WITH SIBLINGS

Parents sometimes find it difficult to manage different limits with different children in the same family, especially if they are younger and don't yet understand the autism. Once the siblings reach age 8 or 9, they are more able to understand the special needs of a sibling on the spectrum, and that can make it easier to explain why you require something different (often perceived as more) from them than from the brother or sister with ASD. Once again, fair is not equal.

I will tell you, with a child on the spectrum, you have to pick your battles. You cannot deal with every issue at once. You have to stay focused on what is most important, or you will lose your control and, in the process, make things more difficult for your child.

I have a client whose family owns a vacation home where several families congregate regularly. Several of the mothers in this group have established the rule that there is to be no eating in the game room. They did this to reduce the mess that they have to clean up at the end of the weekend. They can enforce this with their children because they can get their children to eat at the table with the family, without risking that the child won't eat at all, or that an emotional explosion will disrupt the entire weekend. The mother whose 13-year-old son has autism chooses not to enforce that particular rule; instead, she saves her effort for more important battles with him, such as his taking medication, attending school, doing homework, or showering everyday. Sometimes, the rules and boundaries need to be modified to make them more adaptable for the individual with ASD.

Balancing family needs is tough in the best of situations. When one (or sometimes more than one) of the family members is on the spectrum, the resulting stress increases accordingly. Like other major issues, autism impacts the entire family dynamic and, thus, every individual in the family. Often, siblings need counseling for issues that arise from living with a brother or sister who has autism. Slanting everything to accommodate that individual's needs and neglecting or downplaying the needs of a more self-sufficient child could possibly set up a co-dependent pattern that could lead to long-term difficulties for the siblings.

As important as it is to tailor expectations of your child with ASD, it is equally important to consider the needs of your other family members. Be sure to schedule time to spend with each child individually doing something special that that child really enjoys.

Again, I cannot stress the importance of educating all members of the family about autism. Teach young siblings early on why fair does not always mean equal.

VIDEO GAMES AND "SCREEN TIME"

Parents often ask me why their child is so captivated by video and computer games. This question comes up all the time, so, if you are a parent wondering about it, you're not alone. These electronic games offer children on the spectrum a very unique interplay between themselves and the world.

When you consider the linear thinking of an individual on the spectrum, it makes sense that video games fit that type of thinking. Playing a video game creates a black and white world, one that is completely pattern-driven; there is little, if any, abstract thought required. The computer-generated character shooting at you steps out from behind the same door every time. If you break a rule, what happens? If you step in front of a bullet you die; this will happen each and every time the game is played. Even better, if you do die, with a press of a button you can quickly start another game, every single time. If things aren't going your way, *beep*, start over. You die, *beep*, start over. You make a mistake, *beep*, start over. So, for an individual on the spectrum, playing the game makes sense; it provides a structured experience that is comfortable and predictable.

One of the first video games was PacMan; playing PacMan was a huge fad when I was growing up. In grade school, I remember my buddy telling me that PacMan was at the arcade and I had to go see it. So, I went to the arcade and played PacMan. I didn't play it very often because I wasn't very good at it. I remember one time, watching this older girl play; she was probably on screen 47. At that level, the game is moving so fast that I couldn't even keep up with how she was maneuvering PacMan. I asked her how she did that, and she said, "Don't you have the book?" I thought, "The book to tell me how to eat dots? I don't need that." The book she was talking about showed the pattern to follow on each screen so the ghosts wouldn't eat Pac-Man. She did not see the ghosts the way I saw them when I played. She was just following the patterns she had learned: "I have to go down, I have to turn there, and then I have to go around here." The screens were flying by and she was just sitting there, talking to me and playing the game. I was happy if I made it to the third screen with no distractions.

Video games give children on the spectrum a way to control the environment. The better a player gets at the game, the more success he experiences, and the higher his score becomes; there is a direct correlation between the score and how long one lasts in the game. What is interesting is that these games serve very similar interests for children who do not have autism spectrum disorder. Researchers have found that many troubled youths play video games as a way to make sense of the world; the rules are consistent.

Every video game that exists is patterned (even the interactive ones). The interactive ones are more complex because there are two people involved, but they still work on a patterned format. The interactive games are mostly shooting games now—I guess that is what kids like. So, if I'm playing a shooting game and I start with Level 1, I'm going to have to go into a building and there will be two guys there that I will have to shoot. Every time I go to Level 1, there will be two guys that I have to shoot. Now, if I go to Level 2, there are three guys. Every time I go to Level 2, there will be the same three guys.

Now, I could change the dynamic of the game by having my partner play with me, but there will still be two guys in Level 1 and three guys in Level 2. Do you suppose that's appealing to kids on the spectrum? Yes, and why? Because that is a world that makes sense to them; it is a world that's not gray. I'm behind this rock and I step out. I wonder what is going to happen to me? I will die. I'll try it again. I wonder what is going to happen now. I die. And you know what? This is awesome! Every time I turn this on, the same thing happens. In real life, I walk out my front door into the world and it's different every day. Well, not in the video game. Video games create a world these kids would love to live in because it doesn't get any more linear than that. It's very easy for them to memorize and to focus, so that eliminates a lot of psychological noise in their world.

I remember watching one boy play with his little brother. I think they were playing a game with the character "Mario," and they had to find stars and secret passages. The boy was four years older than his little brother who had autism. He said, "Now, Stevie, where's that star?" "Go up, go over, go down, climb that ladder." "Oh, yeah. Thanks." This kid had played it the same amount of times and was four years older, but Stevie knew where everything was. It was just amazing that he knew that level of detail. Because this is an environment that can be very comfortable for individuals on the spectrum, many of them enjoy it.

I was speaking to one young lady in my office recently about how the brain works and video games. Let me tell you, there is a big difference between girls on the spectrum and boys on the spectrum regarding video games. I'm not saying that the girls don't like the computer, but I rarely have a girl on the spectrum who says, "I LOVE to play Mario Brothers. That's all I want to do." I'm not saying this is always true, but the girls have a tendency to focus more on trying to establish friendships and on boys. Girls have to figure out what they're going to do with their time, their energy, and their focus. Boys tend to focus on the video games. I have boys who will literally play video games, if given the opportunity, 10 to 12 hours per day.

Video and computer games can also calm the autistic player by allowing him to tune out external sensory stimuli. However, playing is not always relaxing because the child can become very stressed if he cannot beat a particular level or must stop playing the game in order to eat dinner.

Although these electronic games often serve the purpose of calming and entertaining the child while allowing him to control the environment and giving him a sense of accomplishment, they also allow the child to avoid social interaction. As with anything, there needs to be balance.

HANDLING HOMEWORK AND HANDWRITING HEADACHES

Homework is a common problem for students with ASD. Think about the amount of stress in their day; it is so hard for them to simply get through the day, let alone handle the added stress of homework when they get home.

Homework presents a number of problems for these kids. Usually, they come home from school mentally drained, and they do not have enough energy to do homework; they are simply too tired. Encourage your child to take a break after school with some type of physical activity. This is good advice for any child, but especially for a child on the spectrum.

Also, these kids think that they shouldn't have to do school work when they aren't at school. Their black and white thinking predisposes them to an aversion to homework. Add to that the executive functioning and organizational difficulties from which they suffer; it is a very complex process to be organized enough to know what assignments are required and when those assignments are due, and to bring home all the materials needed to complete each assignment. Given these factors, it is easy to see how the difficulties caused by autism add up to a recipe for failure when it comes to homework.

We have already described how children can maneuver to fall between the cracks; they tell a parent that homework is at school and tell teachers that the homework is at home. For many parents with kids on the spectrum, this situation is very confusing and frustrating indeed. Homework doesn't even come home. It is nearly impossible to help a child complete homework or hold a child accountable for assignments that can't be identified or accomplished without the proper materials. Many kids do this intentionally to manipulate the situation at home and, thereby, avoid working on their assignments. I see this all the time.

With their lack of intrinsic motivation, these kids know that their parents care much more about the homework than they do. I have seen this become a trap for many parents who, in an effort to teach their child how to do homework and assist him in staying on track at school, end up taking on the responsibility of the work, which is just the way their spectrum child wants it.

One day, in a discussion about homework, a student asked me, "Dr. Wahlberg, how many hours do you work a week?" I told him, then, he followed up with the question, "Okay, what do you do when you get home?" Well, I told him that I check e-mail, eat, and go to bed. He then said to me, "Well, I go to school 36 hours a week, which is pretty much my job. Then, after school, I have to go home and do more work. And I don't even get paid. See, Doctor, you at least get paid!" That was his perspective, and it seems to be common. For individuals on the spectrum to do homework, they need to know what is in it for them. They most likely will need extrinsic motivation. This requires the first/then linear processing. First, 20 minutes of homework, and then 20 minutes of time on the computer, and so on.

In addition, when a child on the spectrum has done his work, he thinks, "done is done," regardless of the accuracy, quality, or level of completion. Asking him to redo it to improve its quality is a concept that is not even on his radar. Since he may not have cared about doing it in the first place, he thinks that he has already made a gargantuan effort, and reworking it is utterly unthinkable. Besides, these children typically don't care about the grade, so providing extrinsic motivation is the only way to get homework of any quality done.

Another issue that relates to homework and warrants mentioning is handwriting. Almost all of the kids I have worked with who are on the spectrum have difficulty with handwriting. Handwriting includes doing homework assignments, especially English, but also copying from the black board, taking notes, etc. Typing or drawing may not be a big problem, but the act of writing, of actually forming the letters with a pencil or pen, may be a cognitive act for a child on the spectrum, rendering it nearly impossible for them to write and listen at the same time. This makes taking notes in class (or relying on notes taken in class for studying) disastrous!

If a child with ASD has handwritten something, and it is not up to the teacher's standard, and the child is asked to rewrite it, he is probably thinking something like, "Are you kidding me? That was so painful there is NO WAY I will rewrite it. There is nothing you could do to me that would get me to do that. You could threaten to take my computer away and I wouldn't redo it."

This can become exasperating for teachers and parents alike. One parent told me that she knew her child could write legibly, but that often the child's handwriting would get messier and the child would refuse to do it. I use this analogy to explain this very situation: Imagine lifting weights at the gym. People usually begin by lifting maybe 25-50 pounds, which is manageable for most. Then, your gym trainer asks you to lift 100 pounds; it's harder, it takes more effort, but it still may be manageable. After a while, you are asked to lift 200 pounds; you struggle with fatigue, sore muscles, and frustration. Would you want to go back to the gym the next day and be asked to lift even more weight?

Now, imagine that just functioning every day—getting through daily tasks—is like lifting that 100 pounds. For most of us, we get through the day a little fatigued maybe, but not exhausted. For children on the spectrum, however, just getting through daily tasks is like lifting 200 pounds; at the end of the day, they are exhausted. Handwriting, for a child on the spectrum, is like lifting 250 to 300 pounds. They have great difficulty writing longhand, which is further complicated because they are not motivated to do it.

One child described it to me by saying that his head and hand each had a brain, and sometimes the brain in his head would tell the brain in his hand to do something, and it would do something different. Imagine the focus it would require to write if you felt that your hands and your brain were at odds. Suffice it to say, handwriting is a major challenge to almost all kids on the spectrum.

Giving individuals on the spectrum options other than writing by hand can make a big difference to their success. Simply reducing the amount of handwriting required will make a difference (e.g., multiple choice questions versus short answers). A few strategies that will ease the writing process for those on the spectrum include: allow them to type on a computer; provide them with notes for the class rather than requiring them to take their own; or provide voice recognition software so they can dictate their assignments. Remember, communicating to the teacher what they know in their heads is what is important, not how that information gets delivered.

Many teachers argue that the child will need these skills in the future to be successful in a career. My response is always, "There is no way that he will choose a career that will require him to use those skills." My focus is always teaching the child how his brain works and giving him strategies for compensating in areas that are a challenge.

Beware of Transition Times

In addition to the lead time and processing time that most people on the spectrum experience, another time issue arises for people with ASD when it comes to change and transition. Remember, the stress we feel when things are changing is multiplied times 10 in someone on the spectrum. New routines, new requirements, and new patterns can be very challenging for kids with spectrum disorders; we need to prepare them before a change is going to happen and then allow them the time they need to adjust to that change. Whether they are going to experience a shift in routine or a move to a new environment, they need time to acclimate, to adjust their thinking.

This is most obvious in school-age children at the end of the school year. Even though a child might hate school, she may have trouble adjusting to summer vacation because of the change in routine. This difficulty with change can make the transition from grade school to middle school, or from middle school to high school, a particularly challenging time.

Middle School

Middle school is one of the most difficult times for a child on the spectrum. Like all other children their age, individuals with autism experience a developing sense of autonomy and independence during these years. They are trying to fit in, thinking about dating, and learning about sex. Most preteens and teens learn these things from their peers or by trial and error. Individuals on the spectrum go through all the same emotional changes without access to a network of friends for support and information. As a result, they learn critical life lessons from television, movies, and the Internet (all of which may be inaccurate at best).

Some research suggests that most of what we gain from grade school and middle school education is social. It's about fitting in, socializing, and processing. Some argue that the majority of educational skills carried over into adulthood—basic reading, writing, and math skills—are learned in kindergarten through grade three.

I could say to anyone reading this book, "Let's go back in time." I have all the testing materials from your second semester as a junior in high school. I'm going to give you all those tests you took then. How would you do? Probably not very well. That doesn't mean you didn't do well in high school.

Have you ever played, "Are You Smarter than a Fifth Grader?" My kids usually win against me. I did just fine in fifth grade, but what did I learn, if I did not retain all of the information that I studied back then? I learned how to function socially, how to fit it, how to do things I did not want to do, and how to respect authority.

In general, what most people learn in school is how to navigate the social environment. Teachers cringe when I say this, but it's not about textbook education for these kids—it's about fitting in, it's about socializing, it's about processing information, and it's about learning to be flexible. Those are some of the lessons we need to teach individuals on the spectrum to help them to be functional.

The student who doesn't want to write an English paper will probably never be required to write an English paper for a job; I can almost guarantee it. Remember the young man who earned a score of 32 on his ACT college entrance exam but was not very functional at work because he turned in employees who bent the rules? He is going to have a job as a chemical engineer and has learned to be more flexible and not to worry so much about others.

During the middle and high school years, parents need to watch out for the "alone time" issue. Spending too much time alone, while it may be relaxing to a child on the spectrum, can be deleterious. Children who are spending time alone are not learning to be social; they are not becoming more flexible by playing video games all day. In fact, they may be going backwards in these areas of development.

Unfortunately, individuals who isolate themselves may struggle with finding jobs and learning independent living skills. Where do you suppose they will end up living? So, it's important that alone time be balanced by activities that stretch the child to learn social skills and interpersonal communications. As I mentioned earlier in this chapter, parents must encourage their child to spend time with friends, especially if the child is introverted. You can use the first/then technique here; first you spend time with friends, then you can spend equal time alone.

BULLYING

Bullying is a big concern for kids on the spectrum. Their odd behavior and lack of social skills often make them targets for bullies at school. The bullying seems to peak in middle school, especially during unstructured time without adult supervision, such as in the gym locker room. I find that, generally, boys tend to seek out others to bully, and girls tend to exclude other girls (obviously not in all cases). Individuals on the spectrum can also misinterpret what is being said to them. Middle schoolers often call each other names in a joking way, although it may not be perceived as such by those on the spectrum.

Bullying is also a big issue on the bus, again because of the lack of adult supervision. For kids who are bullied, this creates a very negative perspective concerning school. It can keep them up at night and create somatic issues with stomachaches, headaches, etc. They really do not want to go to school. The best thing to do with bullies is also the hardest for kids on the spectrum to pull off—that is, to ignore them. Bullies are good at being persistent, and often individuals with ASD cannot ignore them. I find it easiest to teach these children to try to control themselves when they are being bullied, to acknowledge the bully with a comment like, "Whatever," and to move on. This way, the bully realizes he has been heard, and he sees that it is not bothering the student, which, hopefully with time, leads him to move on.

In some cases, gym classes or the bus ride may be too much for a child, so a different option can greatly reduce stress for the student on the spectrum. However, care should be exercised when creating alternative programming. Substituting writing a research paper on racquetball may not be an appropriate alternative to gym class because kids on the spectrum do not like writing and may see this as a punishment.

A couple of years ago, I wrote a letter to excuse a young man who was miserable in his physical education class. The next week, he was almost dancing when he came to my office, he was that excited. He reported that the bullying was gone and, best of all, he got to use the gym period as a study hall, which meant that he did not have as much homework! It was a double win—what a change in his life.

Interestingly, when things improve in their lives, kids seem to experience less bullying, even if the actual level of bullying hasn't changed a great deal. This happens because when they are feeling good, their good box is much larger and, therefore, they are much more accommodating of those around them. In this way, the child's experience of bullying can be used as a barometer for his overall state of mind.

OVERLOAD

Overload happens frequently to kids on the spectrum when they are in a school environment. In reaction to feeling overwhelmed, they express behavioral extremes: overt acting out or shutdown. The kids who are overtly acting out are the easier kids to deal with; those who shut down into their own little world are much harder to reach and much harder to motivate. They seem to have pictures, movies, or songs playing in their heads; it is very easy for them to escape inside themselves, letting their minds go where they want to go.

Sometimes overload occurs in reaction to dealing with circumstances that are gray (i.e., not black and white). I worked with a young man whose high school Spanish teacher would randomly call on students to answer the homework questions. He always had his homework done, and he always knew what he was doing, but the second he walked through those doors, he would feel overloaded to the point where he couldn't process what was being said in the class and he couldn't respond. So, our therapeutic approach was to take something that was gray, and causing serious distraction, and try to make it more black and white. I asked the teacher, "Is there any way that, if you are going to call on this boy, you could tell him the day before which problem you were going to ask him to answer?"

One day, she explained to the boy, "Okay, tomorrow, I'm going to call on you for question number 3. I won't call on you for anything else we do in class, but I will call on you for number 3. Is that okay?" That approach was still stressful for this young man but, at least when he walked through the classroom doors, he knew what was expected of him and, most importantly, when he would be called on. If a child on the spectrum feels that a situation is going to be random, and he doesn't know what is going to happen, his anxiety increases and this can cause him to hit overload.

If I announced to an audience, "Someone has a sticker under the seat, and whoever it is has to join me on stage for a chat. We might talk about some personal issues, but I won't embarrass you too much." How many people would think, "Oh, I hope he's not serious"? Then, each person would feel under his or her chair and think, "Whew! I don't have a sticker so I have nothing to worry about. I can't wait to see what happens because it's not happening to me!" That sense of stress and panic begins to describe what occurs all day long to kids on the spectrum.

Usually, school itself isn't so bad because it's consistent. Classes start at the same time, lunch is at the same time, the teachers are the same every day, etc. However, there are inconsistencies at times. Remember, in middle school and high school, when you had a substitute teacher? What was that like? In my school, that information spread like wildfire. Everyone wanted to know what class the substitute was teaching and tried to find out as much information as possible, because it was perceived as a kind of free class.

I really liked when I had a substitute teacher for band period. I normally played the trumpet, but when we had a substitute, I took advantage of the opportunity and played the drums, which wasn't possible when we were in our regular routine. I could not wait to play the drums. That's what some individuals who don't have autism feel—the excitement of a new experience. Imagine how individuals who have autism feel. It is completely opposite. "I have to go home today." "Why?" "I have to go home today because we have a substitute teacher seventh period. It is not the regular band teacher." What is left unsaid is, "I don't know what to expect, or what will happen, so I can't handle it."

Why does the perspective change so much for children on the spectrum? These children don't like substitutes because they know the band teacher (how he talks, the language he uses, his expectations) and they know his routine (always exactly 10 minutes for warm-up, etc.). A substitute teacher changes the routine and that's a stressor for them. Neuro-typical kids, however, probably think that having a substitute is fun. Remember the rule of thumb—in many cases, what creates positive excitement for the neuro-typical kids creates stress for children with ASD.

Appearing Different in the Classroom

Many individuals with ASD don't want to appear different; expecting them to raise their hands and ask for help is unrealistic. Neuro-typical kids know how to adapt by watching and learning from other students. Individuals on the spectrum don't have that skill and so are often left on their own. The important thing about getting these children to ask for help is that we don't want to draw a lot of attention to them. That's why I encourage teachers to walk around the classroom when they give an assignment, to see if anyone has any questions. I recommend that the teacher ask several students, "Could you please tell me what you are supposed to be doing?" By asking a few of the students, including the child on the spectrum, if they are clear on what they need to be doing, the teacher does not single out any one particular child.

The child might respond, "Yes, we're supposed to be circling the verb." Now, will anyone be able to tell who the child on the spectrum is? No. There will probably be five or six other children in class who don't know what is going on either. But the difference with those kids is that they know how to fake it, or to ask a peer. They look onto someone else's paper to compensate or ask someone else in class what to do. Children on the spectrum don't know how to do this. The walking around technique is a good strategy because the teacher can make sure the students understand the assignment, and the students will be motivated to answer without being put on the spot.

Working with educators, I've had children put on the reward system just for listening to the teacher. So, every time the teacher approaches the student and the child can repeat what the teacher said, the child can earn some "your time" at the end of the day. See how that works? I reward children for listening to a teacher whom they do not want to listen to, because they would rather go into their own little world which is so much more interesting and comfortable than the world we're forcing them to be in. This is much more effective than penalizing a child for bad behavior.

DATING

Dating is a challenge for kids on the spectrum; they talk about dating and they work through dating issues just like everybody else does. As I have mentioned, I facilitate quite a few social groups in my practice. When the kids are younger, the boys and girls meet in separate groups, but when they reach college age and become adults, I integrate them.

The girls in my middle school Asperger's groups all talk about boys and dating. None of them have really dated, but they talk about it. It's not as if there isn't an interest. It's not as if they don't want to be social. It's just a challenge for them. We work on getting over that social barrier; I teach them how to be social.

A few years ago, a young man joined the boys high school group and said that he needed help meeting a girl whom he liked; he wanted to ask her to an upcoming dance. He asked the guys in group for ideas on how he could go about meeting this girl. It was very interesting to hear four guys give their thoughts on meeting girls when none of them had ever done it before. I remember one young man said, "You put your arm on the locker next to her and lean over and give her a kiss on the cheek." Maybe he saw an old episode of "Happy Days" and was referring to how the Fonzie character acted. I was quick to explain that this would not be such a good idea.

Needless to say, we came to the conclusion that he should start by waving to her and eventually just say, "Hi," and introduce himself. We practiced this in group and he did it. He made first contact. With time, and with practice in group, he asked her to the dance, and she said yes! He was like a hero in group; I thought the guys were going to carry him off on their shoulders when the session ended.

He did come in with one issue as the dance approached; he said that he did not know how to dance. One of the guys said, "Make sure you only dance the slow dances because if you dance the fast dances you will look like a dork." (I am not sure where he got this information, but maybe he's not so far off).

Well, the young man said "okay," but he was worried because he did not know how to dance slow dances either. The individual who made the recommendation said, "Stand up and I will show you." I could not believe it! Both young men stood up and began slow dancing in my office! The one said to the other, "Put your hand here, move your feet like this, etc." Of course, he had never been to a dance, but somehow he knew how to dance anyway. These two did this dancing demo in front of the three other guys in group. Guess what they were doing? Taking notes. They were asking questions and trying to learn the slow dance steps. The young man with the date went to the dance and was successful and said that he had a good time; once again he achieved hero status in the group.

He came back a few weeks later, and one of the guys asked him how things were going with the girl from the dance. He responded with, "I hate her." I remember thinking, "Oh, no, what could have happened?" Many thoughts raced through my abstract brain. He explained that he was at a church group and this girl was there. He was standing in a group of young adults right next to her and she did not say, "Hi" to him. I asked if anything else had happened and he said, "No." I asked for more information, and he said that he had planned out what to say to her but, in the plan in his head, she needed to say, "Hi" first to initiate the conversation. I asked him, "What if she felt the same way? Maybe she went home and said to her dad, 'Tom was standing right next to me and never even said hi!'" He replied, "I never thought about it in that way, but I still hate her." He simply could not get over the fact that she disappointed him because she did not say hello first. He did learn how to deal with this issue in future interactions by being more flexible and adjusting his expectations but, once again, the linear thinking of autism took its toll in this social interaction.

Sometimes issues arise when an individual on the spectrum hyper-focuses on a girl, for example, memorizing her schedule in order to see her during the day, which might appear to others as if he is stalking her (this is more obvious if the girl happens to be popular). Part of the problem is that these kids do not blend very easily and often get caught watching or following the girls they like. They need social instruction in order to fit in.

Group sessions fill a critical need for young people who struggle with social acceptance. The group therapy helps them build confidence in their social skills, and, for some, it is the only place where they feel comfortable enough to share their experiences.

CHAPTER 20

CONCLUSION: A NOTE OF HOPE AND ENCOURAGEMENT

Take time to reflect on gains, learn from mistakes, and, most importantly, do not give up. There is a lot of hope for the future.

I hope that this book has served the purpose that I had intended. It's time to move forward and start the journey. There will be ups and downs, but if you follow some of the suggestions in this book, you may find that the ups are higher and the downs are less dramatic and less frequent. Your hard work will increase the probability that your child will develop into a young adult who has the tools to be happy and functional in life.

Begin to assemble a team of people who either understand autism or are willing to learn. Push the envelope, so to speak, with your child, getting him more engaged and active in his environment. Many of these individuals can learn to be functional—it just takes hard work. Remember, they don't have to like it; they just have to do it. I have found over the years that there is no easy route or short cut, but there is no doubt that it can be done. There is more and more information and help available to you.

The level of functioning is relative to each individual on the spectrum. One person's strengths are not the same as another's.

Likewise, the level of intervention that is required is different from individual to individual. Not every child on the spectrum is going to be off-the-charts successful, but that does not mean that the child cannot be happy and functional to some degree. Some individuals on the spectrum may not be able to live alone; they may require adult care, but we still can increase their level of functioning and make them happy. Everyone is unique and different, and the level of functioning is relative. See your child as an individual, set realistic goals for him, and help him strive to achieve those goals. Once they are achieved, set the bar higher. Take time to reflect on gains, learn from mistakes, and, most importantly, do not give up. There is a lot of hope for the future.

Appendix A
Defining Autism

Diagnostic Criteria

Diagnosing a child with autism is a complex process. Clinicians have a manual called the *Diagnostic and Statistical Manual of Mental Disorders – Fourth Edition* (DSM-IV-TR), which is published by the American Psychiatric Association (Washington, DC, 2000). This is the main diagnostic reference for mental health professionals in the U.S. and contains specific guidelines for all mental health diagnoses.

The DSM-IV-TR is used to identify individuals who may have a *clinically significant* area of difficulty that places them outside of what is normally expected. Everyone feels depressed or anxious at times, but clinically significant refers to a condition outside the normal limits. In addition, it implies that the anxiety or depression begins to have a significant impact on one's ability to function. Emotional disorders such as depression, anxiety, and schizophrenia, are examples of disorders that can be diagnosed with the help of the DSM-IV-TR. Criteria for each disorder must be met in order for an individual to be diagnosed with a disorder listed in the DSM-IV-TR.

We assess children in the same way as adults. Do they have an area of difficulty that is significantly different from what is expected for the child to be considered normally functioning? Diagnostic labels are used to indicate commonalities among individuals. The defining symptom of autism that differentiates it from other syndromes and/or conditions is substantial impairment in social interaction. That's it in a nutshell— *substantial impairment in social interaction.* There are no medical tests that can be performed to indicate the presence of autism or any other PDD. A small number of individuals with autism (2% to 6%) have a genetic abnormality called fragile X syndrome which can be detected with DNA testing. Approximately 30% of children with fragile X syndrome have autism. The diagnosis of ASD is based upon the presence or absence of a specific set of behaviors.

STATE AND NATIONAL DIAGNOSTIC CRITERIA AND STATISTICS

The State of Illinois defines autism as follows:

Autism is a lifelong, treatable developmental disability that typically appears during the first three years of life. Autism is four times more prevalent in boys than in girls. It occurs in all socio- economic groups. Specifically, autism is a neurological disorder that interferes with the normal development of the brain. The areas of the brain affected control verbal and non-verbal communication, social interaction, and sensory development. Children with autism often display inappropriate repetitive activities, have difficulty with changes in daily routines and display unusual behavioral responses to sensory experiences. Autism is one of five disorders that fall under the umbrella of Pervasive Developmental Disorders (PDD).

According to the Illinois State Board of Education's 2006 Annual Report, there are 2,111,706 Illinois school children. Of those, 322,541 are special education students and 9,455 students fall under the autism category. Currently, Illinois counts twice as many children with autism in their public schools as they did five years ago. There could be as many as 14,076 children on the autism spectrum in Illinois schools today (1 in 91).

According to the Center for Disease Control, the national average is 1 in 110 children are on the autistic spectrum.

The federal definition states:

The Individuals with Disabilities Education Act [IDEA 300.7 (c)(1)(i)] defines autism as "a developmental disability significantly affecting verbal and nonverbal communication and social interaction, generally evident before age three, that adversely affects a child's educational performance. Other characteristics often associated with autism are engagement in repetitive activities and stereotyped movement, resistance to environmental change or change in daily routine, and unusual responses to sensory experiences. The term autism does not apply if a child's educational performance is adversely affected primarily because the child has an emotional disturbance.

Appendix B
Diagnosing Autism

The Diagnostic Approach

Evaluating if an individual may be on the autism spectrum is a multi-step process. There are a number of instruments available to diagnosticians to evaluate the presence of an autism spectrum disorder (ASD). The following screening instruments are specifically designed to detect symptoms associated with autism spectrum disorders:

1) Checklist for Autism in Toddlers (CHAT)
2) Autism Screening Questionnaire (ASQ)
3) High-Functioning Autism Spectrum Screening Questionnaire (ASSQ)
4) Australian Scale for Asperger's Syndrome (ASAS)

The following checklists and rating scales are also used to help in the specific diagnosis of individuals on the autism spectrum:

1) Childhood Autism Rating Scale (CARS)
2) Autism Behavioral Checklist (ABC)
3) Gilliam Autism Rating Scale (GARS)
4) Gilliam Asperger's Disorder Scale (GADS)
5) Asperger's Disorder Diagnostic Scale

Observational assessment methods can also play a part in the diagnostic process. These include a naturalistic observation of the individual in a number of settings with a number of different individuals. The Autism Diagnostic Observation Schedule (ADOS) is an example of a standardized observation method often used in an evaluation.

Any private evaluation will involve not only a combination of these instruments, but also a clinical interview with the child and family.

Input from the school (if the child is of school age) also plays an important role. The clinician can observe the child in the academic setting, conduct phone interviews with staff from the academic environment, or provide the staff that knows the child best with rating scales to complete, which can be evaluated by the examiner and used as part of the evaluation.

THE REASON TO SEEK A DIAGNOSIS

Many parents wonder if they really need a diagnosis. Obtaining a diagnosis can be expensive, time consuming, and difficult. It can also be a frustrating process, as the symptoms and resulting behaviors are not as clinically conclusive as some other medical diagnoses are. As a result, misdiagnosis for higher functioning individuals can be common at earlier ages, before the clinically significant impact on social behavior is evident. These early diagnoses are usually ADD or ADHD, anxiety disorder, depression, or oppositional defiant disorder (ODD).

I definitely recommend that you pursue a diagnosis from someone who specializes in working with children on the spectrum. Many therapists, although very qualified to work with children on behavioral issues, won't be able to provide the insight and understanding of the reasons behind your child's behavior if they don't have a background in diagnosing and treating autism. This can make all the difference in your child's ability to progress in therapy. I have known families that spent countless months working with therapists without achieving much, only to find out later that working from an emotional perspective was not addressing the core issues of their child on the spectrum. It is important that therapy focuses on teaching families to better understand and communicate with their child on the spectrum, using techniques such as cognitive behavioral interventions, and coming up with a plan for the parents to follow. My clinical experience suggests that this proves more effective than a therapist who engages in play therapy, for example, or talks about emotions.

PERVASIVE DEVELOPMENTAL DISORDER/AUTISM AS A SOCIAL DISABILITY

The term *pervasive* refers to the condition being lifelong; *developmental* refers to dealing with children. Autism is a complex developmental disability that typically appears during the first three years of life and is the result of a neurological disorder that affects the normal functioning of the brain, impacting development primarily in the areas of social interaction and communication skills.

According to the DSM-IV (1994), it is characterized by severe and pervasive impairment in the following areas of development:

Significant impairments in social interactions

Significant impairments in communication abilities

The presence of stereotyped interests, behaviors, and activities

Both children and adults with autism typically show difficulties in verbal and nonverbal communication, social interactions, and leisure or play activities.

Autism is one of five disorders that fall under the umbrella of pervasive developmental disorders (PDD), a category of neurological disorders. The term PDD is widely used by professionals to refer to children with autism and related disorders. However, there is a great deal of disagreement and confusion among professionals concerning the PDD label. According to the DSMV-IV criteria, PDD is not a specific diagnosis, but an umbrella term under which the specific diagnoses are defined.

PDD includes five diagnoses:

1) Autism

2) Asperger's disorder

3) Rett's disorder

4) Childhood disintegrative disorder

5) Pervasive developmental disorder, not otherwise specified.

PERVASIVE DEVELOPMENTAL DISORDERS CHART

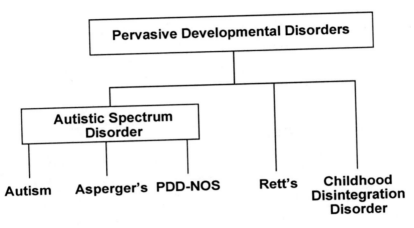

Diagram B-1 - Often, the term autism spectrum disorder (ASD) is used synonymously with the term PDD, though that is not strictly accurate, since Rett's and childhood disintegration disorder may exist without autism. Rett's disorder and childhood disintegration disorder are beyond the purview of this book.

AUTISM

To receive a diagnosis of autism, the individual must meet five diagnostic criteria. First, two aspects of social interaction must be met, which include: 1) a lack of social/emotional reciprocity, which might manifest as a failure to develop peer relationships or lack of seeking to share enjoyment, interests, or achievements; and 2) a marked impairment in use of nonverbal behaviors, which is a significant impairment in communication skills. This would include a delay in, or total lack of, development of spoken language (not accompanied by attempts to compensate), marked impairment in ability to initiate or sustain conversation, stereotyped and repetitive use of language, or a lack of varied, spontaneous make-believe play.

The third criterion for autism involves either an encompassing preoccupation with stereotyped and restricted patterns of interest, nonfunctional routines or rituals, stereotyped and repetitive motor mannerisms (e.g., hand-flapping, finger-flicking, spinning), or persistent preoccupation with parts of objects (what is commonly referred to as stimming).

Fourth, the previous symptoms must be present prior to three years of age to meet the criteria for autism. Finally, a diagnosis of autism cannot be made if the criteria for either Rett's disorder or childhood disintegration disorder are met.

ASPERGER'S DISORDER

Asperger's disorder (sometimes called Asperger's syndrome) shares two of the diagnostic criteria of autistic disorder: 1) a lack of social/emotional reciprocity, which might manifest as a failure to develop peer relationships or lack of seeking to share enjoyment, interests, or achievements; and 2) encompassing preoccupation with stereotyped and restricted patterns of interest, nonfunctional routines or rituals, stereotyped and repetitive motor mannerisms (e.g., hand-flapping, finger-flicking, spinning), or persistent preoccupation with parts of objects. The impairments must impact social, occupational, or other types of functioning. Individuals with Asperger's disorder do not exhibit significant delays in spoken language or cognitive development. A diagnosis of Asperger's disorder cannot be made if criteria are met for another spectrum disorder or for schizophrenia.

PERVASIVE DEVELOPMENTAL DISORDER—NOT OTHERWISE SPECIFIED (PDD-NOS)

There are incidences in which symptoms associated with autism spectrum disorders are present, but all the criteria needed for a single category are not met. For example, the age of onset may be later, the symptoms may be atypical or less severe, or language development may be delayed. When this is the case, a diagnosis of pervasive developmental disorder—not otherwise specified is given.

THE DIFFERENCES BETWEEN AUTISM AND ASPERGER'S DISORDER

There are differences diagnostically between individuals with autism and Asperger's disorder. The most significant difference between the two diagnoses is related to language development. Individuals with autism either do not develop spoken language (about 25% of the cases), or, if they do develop some language (their first 15-20 words), they stop speaking at about 18-24 months of age. At this point, there is not an attempt made by the individual to communicate in another fashion (e.g., gesture, mime, and sign). This is referred to as regressive autism. A small percentage of children on the autism spectrum do develop spoken language, and they engage in *parroting* and/or *echolalia*. Parroting is repeating what is said. For example, ask a child, "Do you want a cookie?" and the child responds with, "Do you want a cookie?" Echolalia refers to when the child repeats phrases, jingles, commercials, etc. that he has heard. This echolalia can be a self-stimulatory behavior for those on the spectrum; it is typically not used as an attempt to communicate.

Individuals with Asperger's disorder commonly learn language from television, computers, or video games. They take the language they have learned from these venues and try to apply it to their social interactions. Typically, individuals with Asperger's disorder are considered higher functioning. Diagnostically, the difference between an individual who meets the criteria for autism and has an average or above average IQ (referred to as high-functioning autism) and an individual with Asperger's disorder comes down to language development.

Some professionals feel that individuals with autism should be classified in a different diagnostic category than those individuals with Asperger's disorder. These professionals believe that there is a difference in the way the brain is affected and in the level of information processing. It is my contention that both individuals with autism and individuals with Asperger's disorder differ from neuro-typical individuals in their ability to process the environment. The greater the difficulty in processing the environment, the more impaired the individual. Regardless of the diagnosis, individuals with both Asperger's and autism experience significant social challenges.

COMMON MISDIAGNOSES (OTHER EXCEPTIONALITIES)

Individuals on the autism spectrum often display behavioral characteristics of other diagnostic categories and, as a result, are often misdiagnosed with other conditions/exceptionalities. In some cases, it is not necessarily a misdiagnosis, but rather the lack of recognition of the autism spectrum. Individuals on the autism spectrum also do have co-morbidity with other clinical disorders; they often do meet the diagnostic criteria for other exceptionalities, which can make diagnosing a challenge. Individuals with autism spectrum disorders can, and do, meet other diagnostic criteria for various conditions/exceptionalities, but in most cases, the diagnosis of ASD is the most thorough, accurate and, therefore, most appropriate way to describe the individual. Some of the most common misdiagnoses are listed below (not in any particular order):

1) Attention deficit disorder/attention deficit hyperactivity disorder (ADD/ADHD)
2) Anxiety
3) Depression
4) Bipolar disorder
5) Schizoid personality disorder
6) Emotional disorder (ED)
7) Obsessive-compulsive disorder (OCD)
8) Social anxiety
9) Nonverbal learning disorder (NVLD)
10) Oppositional defiant disorder (ODD)

Remember, social difficulty is what diagnostically separates individuals on the spectrum from those not on the spectrum. Many of the diagnoses listed above are given until the point when the social component is identified, thus making ASD a more appropriate diagnosis than could be recognized earlier.

At that juncture, the diagnosticians must evaluate if the prevailing condition/exceptionality is autism spectrum disorder, even though an individual may meet the diagnostic criteria of the other diagnostic categories. To render an effective diagnosis, they need to understand how individuals on the autism spectrum struggle in many facets of social, emotional, and academic functioning. It can be particularly difficult to see these factors clearly in very high-functioning individuals, especially if the person conducting the evaluation is inexperienced with autism.

Attention Deficit Disorder/Attention Deficit Hyperactivity Disorder (ADD/ADHD). Those diagnosed as being on the autism spectrum can display the symptomology of ADD or ADHD. They can struggle with focus and hyperactivity. Is this due to boredom, lack of motivation, or sensory issues? Or, is it related to a biological inability to attend? Differentiating between ADHD and autism spectrum requires looking at attentional deficits versus inattention and hyperactivity attributable to the autism spectrum because of joint attention difficulties, an obsessional agenda, a weak drive for central coherence, sensory issues, and/or motivation (see Chapter 2, The Control Theory, for an explanation of central coherence theory). The key to establishing the proper diagnosis is evaluating what is at the root of the difficulty.

Anxiety/Depression. Anxiety and depression can be very prevalent in those on the spectrum because they see the world in a very black and white, linear fashion, and they want things to be the same and consistent. Since the world is not black and white, life for them can be very stressful. This perception that the world is never the way they want it to be leaves them very disappointed and can lead to elevated levels of anxiety and depression.

A great deal of anxiety and depression symptomology can also stem from the lack of meaningful friendships and the social awkwardness experienced by those on the autism spectrum. When evaluating whether an individual suffers from an anxiety disorder or is on the spectrum, certain questions must be answered. Could the anxiety be related to his obsessional preoccupations and/or obsessive worries and the realization that things are rarely the same in life? Is it due to the fact that life is more shades of gray than it is black and white? Is it the result of being inflexible? If so, he may be on the spectrum. Are her social abilities intact, but she struggles with social anxiety in larger groups? Both individuals on the spectrum and those not on the spectrum who suffer from social anxiety will experience social anxiety in general. Diagnostically, those with just social anxiety have at least one same-aged peer with whom they have an appropriate social relationship, in spite of their anxiety in the larger group setting. This is not true for those on the spectrum.

Individuals with ASD do not have intact social abilities. Therefore, they do not typically have appropriate social relationships with same-aged peers, and they struggle in groups (keep in mind the discussion on interacting with older and younger individuals). During the evaluation process, it is also important to get the individual's perspective on what constitutes a friend. Higher-functioning individuals on the autism spectrum typically will report having what they perceive as friends, but no best friend.

Obsessive-Compulsive Disorder (OCD). Many individuals on the autism spectrum can develop obsessive/compulsive traits as a way to control their environment and tune out what is seen as irrelevant or bothersome to them. By doing this, they also reduce anxiety; the more control someone on the spectrum feels they have over the environment, the less the overall anxiety. What is so interesting in those on the autism spectrum is that they seem to make a choice about what context the obsession/compulsions will apply. For example, they may have an obsession with germs, but only in the cafeteria at school and in no other contexts or environments, or an individual on the autism spectrum might have an obsession with wearing cool designer clothes, while at the same time, he neglects his personal hygiene.

In some cases, older individuals diagnosed with obsessive-compulsive disorder realize that their obsession and compulsions are unreasonable or excessive. Individuals on the autism spectrum do not feel that their obsessions are unreasonable or excessive and they want to engage in the obsession/compulsion. They also do not attempt to suppress their obsessive thoughts as is diagnostic for neuro-typical individuals. For those on the spectrum, we also see cognitive rigidity (thinking that is unchangeable), obsessional thinking, and preoccupations as inherent within the diagnosis.

Tic Disorder. When attempting to differentiate between the presence of tic disorder or the autism spectrum, one must assess the presence of a sudden, rapid, recurrent, nonrhythmic, stereotyped movement or vocalizations (tics) in comparison with the repetitive motor/stereotypical movements found in those on the spectrum. These can include hand flapping, spinning, or repeating what they have heard in the past (echolalia).

Schizoid Personality Disorder. Individuals with a diagnosis of schizoid personality disorder display a flat affect, want to be alone, may not pursue friendships but possess social skills, and can function in a group setting but choose not to. Diagnostically, an individual cannot receive a diagnosis of schizoid personality disorder if the criteria are met for a pervasive developmental disorder. Schizoid personality disorder does not have a neurological component as in PDD and the onset occurs by adulthood. The onset for PDD occurs during childhood.

People with schizoid personality disorder can be difficult to differentiate from those with ASD who are introverted and may prefer to be alone. Again, the difference lies in the social ability, in general, with which those on the autism spectrum struggle regardless of desire. Those on the spectrum are also diagnostically impaired in nonverbal communication, and display a pattern of restricted interests or repetitive behaviors.

A diagnosis of schizophrenia requires the individual to suffer, at some point during the illness, from hallucinations (either visual or auditory). At times, individuals on the spectrum may describe hearing voices in their heads. One needs to evaluate if the voices in their heads are actually the individuals talking to themselves, replaying a video, or replaying something that someone in their life has said to them in the past. Their social exceptionality can make it difficult for individuals on the spectrum to appropriately describe what they are hearing or saying in their heads. Individuals on the spectrum can also be highly sensitive to noises and may describe hearing noises at times that can be related to overload and/or their auditory hypersensitivities.

Bipolar Disorder. Individuals on the spectrum change moods very quickly and without an obvious antecedent. That raises the question of whether this is an example of an ultra-rapid bipolar episode or if it is due to the fact that their perception of the way things should be going was not met. Because of their black and white way of processing the world, they see things as either good or bad, not gray. If things do not go the way they want them to, they can get very upset. Not a little upset, but very upset, sometimes escalating into a state of rage. Characteristic of someone on the spectrum, there is no middle ground; there are only the extremes. That's the black and white thinking. They have to get very upset because there is not an in between nor the flexibility in emotion.

The bipolar diagnosis can be given in conjunction with autism spectrum when one can pinpoint a change in mood and level of functioning related to a specific event that can be performed with no issues one day and not performed the next with no antecedent event that precipitates the change. It can also be related to a generally pervasive depressed mood that is followed by an elevated mood. The diagnostician must determine if it could be an ultra-rapid cycle. If this is related to issues for someone on the autistic spectrum, is it volatility and aggression related to not getting their way? Is it anger about a plan and routine that was not followed? This needs to be explored to properly diagnose and differentiate between autism and bipolar disorder or if it is both.

Emotional Disorder (ED). Children diagnosed with ED often struggle with anxiety and depression, or struggle with other emotional challenges. Many individuals on the autism spectrum struggle with anxiety and/or depression inherent within the diagnosis.

Nonverbal Learning Disorder (NLD). A diagnosis of nonverbal learning disorder is given when the individual demonstrates difficulty in motor functions, visual spatial functions, social interactions, and sensory perception. Individuals with NLD score differently on their performance and verbal abilities on a standardized assessment instrument, scoring higher on the verbal portion of the test. IQ tests are split between verbal and performance tests; the consolidation of the two results in a full-scale IQ score. Some researchers consider distinguishing between nonverbal learning disorder and Asperger's disorder as splitting hairs, because, diagnostically, people with either of these disorders experience social challenges. Choosing one over the other may not be so relevant when looking at interventions, although NLD diagnoses reveal the cognitive challenges these individuals face. In either case, people with these disorders struggle with social interactions.

Oppositional Defiance Disorder (ODD). Those working with individuals on the spectrum may say that they will not follow the rules, they talk back, they do not respect authority, and they do their own thing; in many cases, these individuals are diagnosed with oppositional defiant disorder or an emotional disturbance. Again, one needs to ask why the behavior is occurring. For those on the autism spectrum, the aforementioned behaviors can be related to their social difficulties, their black and white linear thinking, and their lack of intrinsic motivation. All behavior has a purpose, and part of the diagnostic process is figuring out the purpose of the behavior and its antecedent. Sometimes we cannot determine the purpose or identify the antecedent event—this does not mean one does not exist. Many individuals on the autism spectrum are diagnosed with ODD because they do not follow the rules and, at times, do not respect authority. Remember, they have a social disability and oftentimes do not see the relevance in doing what others are doing or in following the rules. In many cases, they do not recognize a hierarchical relationship with authority figures like parents and school personnel. They may not listen and will want to do things their own way, which obviously appears defiant and oppositional.

Sensory Integration Disorder (SID). SID implies that the individual has difficulty processing the sensory environment and struggles with regulating his sensory processing system. Where does sensory integration disorder fit in? I believe all children on the spectrum have a problem processing the environment. Sensory integration disorder is differentiated from autism spectrum disorder by the social challenge. Those who have SID and are very capable socially cannot be on the autism spectrum. There is not a diagnostic category related to sensory integration disorder available to psychologists in the DSM-IV-TR. I do see many clients with SID who would fall on the autism spectrum because they also have the social disability.

Dual Diagnoses

Children on the spectrum can have dual diagnoses. Diagnostically, we must evaluate if autism spectrum disorder provides us with additional information needed to best facilitate treatment for the individual. In many cases, we gain further information about the emotional profile of an individual with the dual diagnosis as it highlights the severity of the level of anxiety, depression, obsessional tendencies, etc. Therefore, they can be helpful and increase diagnostic accuracy.

Diagnosis of Higher Functioning Individuals

Higher functioning individuals on the autism spectrum can be a challenge to identify prior to middle school. The distinguishing characteristic among those on the autism spectrum is their social disability and the lack of social skills needed to be functional both academically and emotionally. This can be difficult to evaluate prior to the fourth or fifth grade.

In some cases, individuals with strong cognitive intellect (the ability to think) are able to compensate for their social inadequacies until the social strain becomes too hard to manage. This usually manifests itself in middle school for a number of reasons. At this point in their emotional development, the social gap is very easy to see as children begin to go through puberty and start to develop a sense of autonomy, or self. At the same time, more is asked of children as they enter middle school. They are faced with more responsibility, many different teachers, changing classrooms, use of lockers, etc. These factors can also create more stress for those on the spectrum, which exacerbates the social inadequacies that were not as apparent prior to middle school.

OTHER FACTORS THAT IMPACT DIAGNOSIS

Other personality factors can impact diagnosis. For example, the child's level of introversion and extraversion plays a role. Those who are introverted can be harder to identify because they do not want to be social, they are more withdrawn, are generally quiet as they do not want to draw attention to themselves, and they may not be bothered by their lack of friends. They would actually prefer to be alone. Those who are extroverted, however, do want friends, are generally more outgoing, and often say and do things that alienate them in their social environment. This may make them more of a target for bullies. In addition, the extrovert on the spectrum may make inappropriate social contact, for example, calling someone they perceive as a friend 50 times after school because that person said hello to them in the hall that day. They may try humor to interact with their peers, not understanding that they may be laughed at, not laughed with. These are just some of the additional factors that complicate the diagnostic process.

APPENDIX C

By A. Heredia, M.D.

MEDICATION TREATMENT IN THE AUTISTIC SPECTRUM DISORDERS

A specific cause of the autism spectrum disorders has not been identified and this has stymied the development of a specific medication to treat all of the impairments and symptoms of the spectrum disorders. Despite the lack of a medication to cure these disorders, medications can be very helpful in the treatment of certain symptoms in autism disorder, Asperger's disorder, and pervasive developmental disorder, not otherwise specified (PDD-NOS).

The symptoms that are potentially amenable to treatment with a medication include volatility, agitation, and mood swings, as well as any manifestation of obsessional thinking such as restricted areas of interests or obsessional preoccupations and obsessional rigidity/inflexibility. Also included in these treatable symptoms are stereotyped behaviors.

Symptoms of inattention, with or without hyperactivity, and impulsivity, whether secondary to a coexisting diagnosis of attention deficit hyperactivity disorder (ADHD) with Asperger's disorder, or attributable to autistic disorder, frequently respond to treatment with medication.

Various medications have been studied and/or used over the past several decades in the treatment of the autistic spectrum disorders. Since this is not an exhaustive discussion of pharmacotherapy of the spectrum disorders, it is best to mention the most relevant medications, or rather, the medications that most consistently have been shown to be helpful in the various symptoms of the autistic spectrum disorders.

The selective serotonin reuptake inhibitors such as Prozac, Zoloft, Lexapro, and Paxil can be helpful in the treatment of restricted areas of interests and obsessional preoccupations as well as obsessional rigidity and inflexibility. They can also improve stereotyped behaviors and some degree of agitation or anxiety that is attributable to over stimulating or overwhelming environments.

The neuroleptics, commonly known as the atypical antipsychotics, such as Risperdal, Abilify, Zyprexa, Seroquel, and Geodon, have been shown to be effective in the treatment of aggression and agitation, self-injurious behavior, stereotyped behaviors, and some of the rigidity.

The psychostimulants are, of course, the medications of choice for ADHD, whether the ADHD is co-morbid with Asperger's disorder, or the inattention with or without hyperactivity/impulsivity is attributable to autistic disorder. Other medications that can treat the symptoms of ADHD in either clinical scenario, such as Strattera, the tricyclic antidepressants, and Wellbutrin, are appropriate options. In addition, other medications which are also used to treat ADHD are clonidine (Catapres), guanfacine (Tenex) (Intuniv). These can reduce agitation and hyperactivity in the spectrum disorders.

Various other medications have shown benefit with specific symptom complexes. For example, some medications have been studied and have shown some benefits in improving organization and planning. A good example of these medications are medications that were originally developed to treat dementia in Alzheimer's disease; donepezil (Aricept), memantine (Namenda), and galantamine (Razadyne). Other medications, such as some anti-seizure medications, have also been shown to be helpful with aggression and irritability. Examples of these are valproate (Depakote), carbamazepine (Tegretol), topiramate (Topamax).

The use of medications in the treatment of the autistic spectrum disorders can be very helpful and, in many cases, life-changing. However, in many cases benefits are meaningful though modest. Significantly, responses to medications can vary much more often in the autistic spectrum disorders and in ways that are not regularly seen by those inexperienced with the spectrum disorders. It is important that a clinician who will be prescribing medication be experienced in the evaluation and treatment of the pervasive developmental disorders.

ACKNOWLEDGEMENTS

I could not have completed this book without the help of a team of talented people including: Jeanne Beard, who pushed me to start this project, and who spent countless hours making sense of my notes and presentation transcripts; my editor, Deb McKew, who could see the big picture while focusing on the many details required to get the job done; and my office manager, Denise Shibona, who keeps me organized. In addition, I want to thank my professional partner, Angel, for writing the Appendix on medications; he has also been a valuable resource in our work at the Prairie Clinic. Last, but surely not least, I would like to thank everyone who agreed to read my manuscript and provide critical feedback during the final stages of writing.

THE PRAIRIE CLINIC
Geneva, Illinois
www.theprairieclinic.com

The Prairie Clinic was founded in 2007 through the vision of Dr. Timothy Wahlberg and Dr. Angel Heredia, each of whom desired to offer individuals and families a broader continuum of services in both the medical and clinical aspects of treatment. The clinic operates on the guiding principal that medical treatment and cognitive behavioral therapy together, in a team approach, benefit the client and maximize results.

The clinic offers psychiatric medical intervention as well as both private and group therapy for individuals.

Dr. Wahlberg is currently involved in on-going research and is developing new research projects to further understand the unique dynamics of individuals on the spectrum. To learn more about this work, please contact the Prairie Clinic at www.theprairieclinic.com.

Timothy J. Wahlberg, Ph.D., is a licensed clinical psychologist and a certified school psychologist. He earned his doctorate degree at Northern Illinois University. Dr. Wahlberg has experience in school and university settings, psychiatric facilities, community mental health centers, as well as private practice. He has published extensively on the subjects of autism and neurological impairments and is involved in several ongoing research projects of related topics. He has spoken at local and national levels on autism and reflex-delay disorder and has conducted a number of training seminars in these areas. Dr. Wahlberg is a member of the American Psychological Association.

Angel Heredia, M.D., is a child and adolescent psychiatrist who received his medical degree and completed his residency at the University of Illinois. He completed his fellowship at Northwestern University Medical School and Children's Memorial Hospital. He is board certified in child and adolescent psychiatry as well as in adult psychiatry by the American Board of Psychiatry and Neurology. Dr. Heredia's expertise is in evaluation and treatment of a wide spectrum of psychiatric problems including attention deficit/hyperactivity disorder, mood and anxiety disorders, obsessive-compulsive disorder, and pervasive development disorders.

CPSIA information can be obtained
at www.ICGtesting.com
Printed in the USA
FSOW02n2210100216
16814FS